Studies in the Book of Hosea

# DOOR of HOPE

D1218422

# CROWN
## CHRISTIAN
## PUBLICATIONS
### Royal Reading

FAITHfortheFAMILY.com

# DOOR of HOPE

## CLARENCE SEXTON

### FIRST EDITION
COPYRIGHT
DECEMBER 2008

CROWN
CHRISTIAN
PUBLICATIONS
*Royal Reading*

FAITH*for the*FAMILY.com

# PILLAR AND GROUND OF THE TRUTH
## SUNDAY SCHOOL AND BIBLE TEACHING SERIES

# DOOR OF HOPE
Copyright © 2008
Crown Christian Publications
Powell, Tennessee · 37849
CrownChristianPublications.com
FAITH*forthe*FAMILY.*com*

ISBN: 978-1-58981-462-2

Layout by Ryan Keiter & Stephen Troell

Printed in the United States of America

# *Dedication*

---

This book is affectionately dedicated to all those in the Lord's family who make it their ministry to encourage others in the wonderful work of the Lord.

*Clarence Sexton*

*Acts 5:42*

# Introduction

The study of the book of Hosea is a very serious and sobering study, but it brings us to a *"door of hope."*

God reminds us that in times of affliction, people seek the Lord. I pray that we are on the threshold of a mighty, heaven-sent revival.

May the fresh wind of the Holy Spirit blow holy fire in our hearts and across our land.

# Contents

# CHAPTER ONE

# GOD'S MESSAGE THROUGH HOSEA

he Creator God chose to reveal His loving heart through His prophet Hosea. Striking parallels can be drawn when we compare ancient Israel to modern America.

Hosea delivered the Lord's message to the northern kingdom, Israel. He was the prophet for the zero hour in the nation of Israel. What the weeping prophet Jeremiah was to Judah, the southern kingdom, Hosea was to the northern kingdom nearly a century and a half later.

Through the troubles in Hosea's home, he reached the consciousness of his calling. Hosea married Gomer in good faith, but her unfaithfulness and ultimate enslavement broke the heart of her husband. Gomer's adultery pictured Israel's apostasy.

In the first three chapters, the story of Hosea's home life sets the stage for understanding God's relationship with His people. The prophet, through the heartbreak of his own marriage, comes to see in a more meaningful way Israel's sin against God. Hosea represents God, our loving heavenly Father. Gomer represents the nation of

Israel and the people of that nation. The Lord's message for each one of us is the message of His love and our responsibility.

Entering this book of the Bible brings us into the heart of God. Hosea 1:1-11 says,

> *The word of the LORD that came unto Hosea, the son of Beeri, in the days of Uzziah, Jotham, Ahaz, and Hezekiah, kings of Judah, and in the days of Jeroboam the son of Joash, king of Israel. The beginning of the word of the LORD by Hosea. And the LORD said to Hosea, Go, take unto thee a wife of whoredoms and children of whoredoms: for the land hath committed great whoredom, departing from the LORD. So he went and took Gomer the daughter of Diblaim; which conceived, and bare him a son. And the LORD said unto him, Call his name Jezreel; for yet a little while, and I will avenge the blood of Jezreel upon the house of Jehu, and will cause to cease the kingdom of the house of Israel. And it shall come to pass at that day, that I will break the bow of Israel in the valley of Jezreel.*

> *And she conceived again, and bare a daughter. And God said unto him, Call her name Loruhamah: for I will no more have mercy upon the house of Israel; but I will utterly take them away. But I will have mercy upon the house of Judah, and will save them by the LORD their God, and will not save them by bow, nor by sword, nor by battle, by horses, nor by horsemen.*

> *Now when she had weaned Loruhamah, she conceived, and bare a son. Then said God, Call his name Loammi: for ye are not my people, and I will not be your God.*

*Yet the number of the children of Israel shall be as the sand of the sea, which cannot be measured nor numbered; and it shall come to pass, that in the place where it was said unto them, Ye are not my people, there it shall be said unto them, Ye are the sons of the living God. Then shall the children of Judah and the children of Israel be gathered together, and appoint themselves one head, and they shall come up out of the land: for great shall be the day of Jezreel.*

This book of the Bible is divided into fourteen chapters. We find a natural division between the first three chapters and chapters four through fourteen. This is God's message given through His messenger Hosea to His ancient people Israel. I give you a warning as we enter into this study—if you see the message of this book only as God speaking to a nation and fail to apply it to the individual, then you will miss the great truth God has for you.

In Hosea's day, God's people were divided into two kingdoms. Ten tribes made up the northern kingdom called Israel, and two tribes made up the southern kingdom called Judah. Hosea's message was given as the northern kingdom stood on the threshold of captivity. They would be dispersed at the hands of their Assyrian captors. Later, the southern kingdom of Judah would fall to the Babylonians. This prophet Hosea preached to Israel telling them that Israel had become a nation with no truth. Let us all understand that we may possess many things, but without truth, we are certainly not going to be what God would have us to be.

Let us begin where the Lord begins this message. In this book, the Lord immediately introduces us to Hosea and his family. As we become acquainted with this family, we are going to discover God's message to each of us. Of course, there is a national emphasis to Israel, but the application is to the individual.

13

# HOSEA

Verse one begins, *"The word of the LORD that came unto Hosea."* This is a defining statement. God's Word came to Hosea, and when God spoke to him, he was obedient. Hosea points us to our loving God.

> *God's redeeming love seeks sinners. It should not be difficult for us to recognize that when God came seeking you and me, He did not come after some great prize.*

The Lord gives us the particular setting and time. Hosea 1:1 says, *"The word of the LORD that came unto Hosea, the son of Beeri, in the days of Uzziah, Jotham, Ahaz, and Hezekiah, kings of Judah, and in the days of Jeroboam the son of Joash, king of Israel."* We know the time and place in which this story comes to pass. This is the amazing story of God's redeeming love.

An author named Graham Scroggie has written a wonderful Bible survey book entitled *The Unfolding Drama of Redemption.* Mr. Scroggie refers to the Bible as God's unfolding drama of redemption. It is! When we open our Bibles, we see God at work in this unfolding drama of redemption.

Early in the Garden, when man sinned against God, it was God who came in the cool of the day crying out, "Adam, Adam, where art thou?" When man sinned against God, God provided a way of salvation and the promise of the Redeemer in shedding the blood of the innocent. In the skins made for Adam and Eve, we see the death of the innocent for the guilty.

As we follow the Bible through, we find this scarlet thread of the blood of Jesus Christ pointing us to Calvary. When God's people were in bondage in Egypt, the blood was placed on the door, and the

14

death angel passed over. God revealed again this unfolding drama of redemption. However, there is no place in the Old Testament where we find such a vivid picture of God's redeeming love as we do in this book of Hosea.

The Bible says in verse two, *"The beginning of the word of the Lord by Hosea. And the Lord said to Hosea, Go, take unto thee a wife of whoredoms and children of whoredoms: for the land hath committed great whoredom, departing from the Lord."* Three times in one verse the Bible uses this word *"whoredom"* meaning repeated sexual sin. Fourteen times we find this expression throughout the book of Hosea. God said to this godly man, *"Go, take unto thee a wife of whoredoms."* His wife will prove to be unfaithful.

One of the great problems that commentators try to solve in this book of the Bible is whether or not God commanded Hosea to take a wife who was already engaged in whoredom, or to take a wife that would become engaged in this type of behavior. The fact remains that God revealed to Hosea that this is what his wife would become, even if she were not already engaged in this type of sinful behavior.

If you are thinking, "It is hard for me to imagine that God would command a man to do that," remember, Hosea is a picture of our God. When we look at the life of Hosea, we are to see our Lord. The Bible says in John 3:16, *"For God so loved the world, that he gave his only begotten Son, that whosoever believeth in him should not perish, but have everlasting life."* God's redeeming love seeks sinners. It should not be difficult for us to recognize that when God came seeking you and me, He did not come after some great prize. He came after sinful people who could not make their own way to God. The only hope we had was for our God to love us and seek after us.

God is going to allow this good man Hosea to live through a great tragedy, to seek after his own wife in unseemly places, to cry out for her in dens of iniquity, and to bring her food and supplies when

15

she is starving at the hands of her lovers. We are going to see him seeking and seeking until he finds her. With every move of this book of the Bible, as this man seeks after his wife, we get a glimpse of our God who loves us *"so"* much that He *"gave His only begotten Son."*

# GOMER

Next, let us consider Gomer, Hosea's wife. Hosea's name means "salvation"; Gomer's name means "completeness." It seems she does everything but complete. She is a woman who engages in the most abominable behavior. She gives her life to the most disgusting things. The Bible says that she is engaged in whoredoms. She forsakes her husband and her children to go after other men, yet Hosea loves her. Nothing is as powerful as the seeking love that God has for us.

Jeremiah 31:3 says, *"The LORD hath appeared of old unto me, saying, Yea, I have loved thee with an everlasting love: therefore with lovingkindness have I drawn thee."* Take special notice of the expression that God has loved us *"with an everlasting love."* God's love for us was never initiated; it had no beginning. He loves us with an everlasting love. There is nothing we can do to make God stop loving us; there was nothing we could do to make God start loving us. God's love is pictured in the love Hosea had for his wife Gomer. Every time you think about her vile behavior, think of what God says concerning you and me and His great love for us.

We read again of God's love in John 13:1, *"Now before the feast of the passover, when Jesus knew that his hour was come that he should depart out of this world unto the Father, having loved his own which were in the world, he loved them unto the end."* He did not stop loving them! When we read the book of Hosea and discover the behavior of Gomer, we find that there was every reason to tell this man, "Why don't you find someone else? Why don't you cast her out and be done with her!" But that is not his love, and that is not the behavior of the love of God. As we look at Gomer, we see ourselves. Our rebellious hearts are laid bare.

We have been conquered by Calvary. The love of Christ constrains us. There was a time in all of our lives when someone could have said, "I do not see what anyone sees in him." But still God loves us.

If you visited the home of Hosea, and you found out that Gomer was that kind of wife, you would not want to eat at her table. As a decent person, you would not want to make friends with her. But, oh dear friend, every one of us is seen in her. She is loved as we are loved with an everlasting love. This is God's message to us.

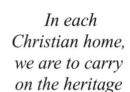

*In each Christian home, we are to carry on the heritage of the Lord.*

We grow so weary and impatient with people. We are such respecters of persons! God spoke here to His ancient people Israel about their sin, their behavior, their idolatry, and their spiritual whoredoms. He is also speaking to us. The Bible says in Isaiah 53:6, *"All we like sheep have gone astray; we have turned every one to his own way; and the LORD hath laid on him the iniquity of us all."*

Occasionally, I meet missionaries who say, "I am going to a certain part of the world because people are so needy; they have never heard the truth, and I want to love them and help them and point them to Jesus." A few years later, we meet those same missionaries, and they have returned from the mission field. It is not loving those people that keeps them there, because they find out that those people have hearts like every other human being—just as black as the charred walls of hell. It is not the people's good behavior that keeps the missionary there. It is the love of Christ, loving lost sinners like you and me. We go for God. We stay for God. Our work is done for Him, not them. Of course we love people; but we love the people because God has conquered our hearts with His love.

We read in Romans 3:9-19,

> *What then? are we better than they? No, in no wise: for we have before proved both Jews and Gentiles, that they are all under sin; as it is written, There is none righteous, no, not one: there is none that understandeth, there is none that seeketh after God. They are all gone out of the way, they are together become unprofitable; there is none that doeth good, no, not one. Their throat is an open sepulchre; with their tongues they have used deceit; the poison of asps is under their lips: whose mouth is full of cursing and bitterness: their feet are swift to shed blood: destruction and misery are in their ways: and the way of peace have they not known: there is no fear of God before their eyes. Now we know that what things soever the law saith, it saith to them who are under the law: that every mouth may be stopped, and all the world may become guilty before God.*

As we look at Gomer and her behavior, we see ourselves. When we look at Hosea and see love, we see our God.

# THE CHILDREN

We have met the man and his wife; now let us meet the children. There are three children in this family. Each of them brings a message from God to us. It is God's message. It is primarily, in interpretation, God's message to Israel, but do not allow this to hinder God's Word from your heart. The people are about to go into Assyrian captivity and be scattered throughout the earth. Even to this day, they are scattered from Nazareth to New York.

My wife and I have two sons, two beautiful daughters-in-law, and six wonderful grandchildren. They love the Lord and are a tremendous joy to us. The family is God's design. In each Christian home, we are to carry on the heritage of the Lord. What sadness we find when this is not the case! The Bible says in Hosea 1:3-5,

> *So he went and took Gomer the daughter of Diblaim; which conceived, and bare him a son. And the LORD said unto him, Call his name Jezreel; for yet a little while, and I will avenge the blood of Jezreel upon the house of Jehu, and will cause to cease the kingdom of the house of Israel. And it shall come to pass at that day, that I will break the bow of Israel in the valley of Jezreel.*

Meet the oldest child of Hosea and Gomer, whose name is Jezreel. Hebrew names are extremely significant. *Jezreel* means "scattered." He says, "My name is 'Scattered.'"

God says, "I am going to scatter my people; I am going to judge my people. I am going to judge this nation." His name declares God's message, "I am going to scatter my people. They are going to suffer defeat and be captured by the Assyrians and dispersed throughout the world."

So what does it mean to meet this boy? It means that they could have been obedient to God and have been blessed. They could have been the objects of God's favor. But not now. They are going to be scattered and not blessed.

Let us apply this to your life and mine. It is our God's passionate desire to bless

*We go for God. We stay for God. Our work is done for Him, not them. Of course we love people; but we love the people because God has conquered our hearts with His love.*

us and our families and to bring us together to do a mighty work in the lives of His people. But when we allow sin to enter in, when we go our own way and not God's way, we cannot be blessed and used of God. We are scattered and defeated and weakened. That is the message this first child brings to us.

The Lord continues His introduction of the children. The Bible says in Hosea 1:6-7,

> *And she conceived again, and bare a daughter. And God said unto him, Call her name Loruhamah: for I will no more have mercy upon the house of Israel; but I will utterly take them away. But I will have mercy upon the house of Judah, and will save them by the LORD their God, and will not save them by bow, nor by sword, nor by battle, by horses, nor by horsemen.*

Next, we meet this little girl. We ask her what her name is, and she says, "Loruhamah." Now, when we saw the boy, the boy looked a lot like his father. We really do not know about this daughter. She may or may not resemble her father; we are not sure whether or not Hosea is her father. But when we hear her Hebrew name, we know God's message to us.

What she says to us is that God will no longer have pity or mercy. He will no longer have this intimate fellowship and relationship that He desires to have with us. Something has happened!

Our God desires for us to be near Him. He wants to bless us, have mercy upon us, pity us, and meet our needs. He wants us to have a relationship with Him that we have with no other. But when sin comes in, that sin prohibits God from having that kind of relationship and fellowship with His people.

God desired to have this kind of crowning, intimate relationship with Israel, but because there was sin and spiritual adultery, that relationship became impossible. Hosea and his wife and children were living examples of what happened nationally. One family displayed what was happening to an entire nation. This daughter's name tells us that God will no longer have mercy and pity upon His children. The tenderness and intimacy is gone.

Some of you once walked with God and had such close communion with God, but now your Christian life is all mechanical. You have all the right answers, and you show up at the right places, but there is no life or real intimacy in your walk with God. This is the message Loruhamah brings to us.

There is a third child born as a result of whoredom. The Bible says in Hosea 1:8-9, *"Now when she had weaned Loruhamah, she conceived, and bare a son. Then said God, Call his name Loammi: for ye are not my people, and I will not be your God."* If you come to the house when this son is born and look at him, you notice something right away. He does not look at all like his father. You look at Hosea and wonder, "Is this really his son? There is no family resemblance here!" The reason for this is that it is not his son. This

*Our God desires for us to be near Him. He wants to bless us, have mercy upon us, pity us, and meet our needs. He wants us to have a relationship with Him that we have with no other.*

is the offspring of an adulterous relationship. The son bears no resemblance to the man that was supposed to be his father. God says, "Give him a name. When he says his name, his name says that he does not belong to Me."

God declares to His people, "My heart's desire is to be your God and for you to be my people; but because of your sin, you are not my people." Of course this troubles people when they are thinking about the Jews. Did God disinherit His people? No, the promise God made to Abraham He will keep. But they are set aside. They do not know God as their Father in their present blindness. They do not know God the way He desires them to know Him.

*A Christian can behave in such a way that he passes down a godly heritage, or he can behave in such a way that there is no godly heritage to pass on.*

Many people in some way identify with the name of Jesus, and yet bear no evidence of being a Christian. There are many people who will say when pressed, "Oh, I have made a profession of faith. Sure! There was a time when I trusted Christ." But they look nothing like a believer in the way they live. This is what we find when we come to Hosea's home. What a shame! The mother could have behaved in such a way that the children could have rejoiced in the heritage handed to them, but she did not. Remember, the mother represents you and me.

A Christian can behave in such a way that he passes down a godly heritage, or he can behave in such a way that there is no godly heritage to pass on. It is a serious matter to say that you are a Christian and not live like a Christian.

God is laying the groundwork for this entire book in this first chapter as we are introduced to the family of Hosea. Hosea's name means salvation; Gomer means completion, and these children's names mean scattered, no mercy, and not my people.

Hosea................................................................Salvation

Gomer................................................................Completion

Jezreel................................................................Scattered

Loruhamah...........................................................No Mercy

Loammi..........................................................Not My People

The Lord does not leave us here. In Hosea 1:10, the Bible says,

> *Yet the number of the children of Israel shall be as the sand of the sea, which cannot be measured nor numbered; and it shall come to pass, that in the place where it was said unto them, Ye are not my people, there it shall be said unto them, Ye are the sons of the living God.*

Notice that little word *"yet"* in the beginning of this verse. This is one of the great "yets" of the Bible. You see, God does keep His promises. He knows the promises that He has made. The Bible says in Genesis 12:1-3,

> *Now the LORD had said unto Abram, Get thee out of thy country, and from thy kindred, and from thy father's house, unto a land that I will shew thee: and I will make of thee a great nation, and I will bless thee, and make thy name great; and thou shalt be a blessing: and I will bless them that bless thee, and curse him that curseth thee: and in thee shall all families of the earth be blessed.*

God says, "With all of this, you are going to be set aside. You are going to be carried captive. You are going to be scattered like the wind, *'Yet the number of the children of Israel shall be as the sand of the sea, which cannot be measured nor numbered; and it shall come to pass, that in the place where it was said unto them, Ye are not my people, there it shall be said unto them, Ye are the sons of the living God.'*"

God is going to bring this to pass someday. Hosea 1:11 says, *"Then shall the children of Judah and the children of Israel be gathered together, and appoint themselves one head, and they shall come up out of the land: for great shall be the day of Jezreel."*

The Spirit of God gave Peter this message when he wrote in I Peter 2:9-10,

> *But ye are a chosen generation, a royal priesthood, an holy nation, a peculiar people; that ye should shew forth the praises of him who hath called you out of darkness into his marvellous light: which in time past were not a people, but are now the people of God: which had not obtained mercy, but now have obtained mercy.*

What a precious promise! You may say, "My life has fallen apart. I am so far removed from God and the things of God." I want you to know that at this moment you may not be a people, but God can make you His people! He can show you His mercy! This is the story of God's redeeming love.

God is speaking to you and me by His great love. The most powerful message for mankind is the love of God. His grace is greater than all our sin. Where sin abounded, grace did much more abound.

> *The most powerful message for mankind is the love of God. His grace is greater than all our sin.*

I do not think I will ever forget the personal testimony given by Dr. Richard Dion. Dr. Dion is a personal friend and faithful pastor in Great Falls, Montana. I share his testimony with you, though it reveals some very personal matters, because He has taken the liberty to tell it publicly.

Pastor Dion said that he was born to a woman out of wedlock. He had no father. He took the name of Richard Griffin. But his loving mother met a good man, who became

24

a godly man, by the name of Dion. Dr. Dion said, "I remember the day as a boy when my mother and stepfather took me to a courthouse. I will never forget going into the courthouse with no father and the name Richard Griffin. But when I came out, I had a father, and my name was Richard Dion."

There was a day when I had no heavenly Father; but someone walked me into a little room and took the Bible and showed me that Jesus Christ died and rose again to save me from my sins. I asked God to forgive my sin, and I believed on the Lord Jesus Christ. I went in that room a lost, hell-deserving sinner. But after trusting the Lord Jesus Christ as my Saviour, I came out of that little room with a heavenly Father and with my name written in the Lamb's Book of Life. I came to know the story of God's redeeming love.

# CHAPTER TWO

# DOOR OF HOPE

The message of hope is the message of the Bible. Our hope is in the Lord. For this reason, God's children are the most hopeful people on earth.

The book of Hosea is the divine love story lived out in the life of the prophet Hosea, his wife Gomer, and their three children. God provides this human display of His great love for us.

Hosea 2:1-23 says,

> *Say ye unto your brethren, Ammi; and to your sisters, Ruhamah. Plead with your mother, plead: for she is not my wife, neither am I her husband: let her therefore put away her whoredoms out of her sight, and her adulteries from between her breasts; lest I strip her naked, and set her as in the day that she was born, and make her as a wilderness, and set her like a dry land, and slay her with thirst. And I will not have mercy upon her children; for they be the children of*

*whoredoms. For their mother hath played the harlot: she that conceived them hath done shamefully: for she said, I will go after my lovers, that give me my bread and my water, my wool and my flax, mine oil and my drink.*

*Therefore, behold, I will hedge up thy way with thorns, and make a wall, that she shall not find her paths. And she shall follow after her lovers, but she shall not overtake them; and she shall seek them, but shall not find them: then shall she say, I will go and return to my first husband; for then was it better with me than now. For she did not know that I gave her corn, and wine, and oil, and multiplied her silver and gold, which they prepared for Baal.*

*Therefore will I return, and take away my corn in the time thereof, and my wine in the season thereof, and will recover my wool and my flax given to cover her nakedness. And now will I discover her lewdness in the sight of her lovers, and none shall deliver her out of mine hand. I will also cause all her mirth to cease, her feast days, her new moons, and her sabbaths, and all her solemn feasts. And I will destroy her vines and her fig trees, whereof she hath said, These are my rewards that my lovers have given me: and I will make them a forest, and the beasts of the field shall eat them. And I will visit upon her the days of Baalim, wherein she burned incense to them, and she decked herself with her earrings and her jewels, and she went after her lovers, and forgat me, saith the* LORD.

*Therefore, behold, I will allure her, and bring her into the wilderness, and speak comfortably unto her. And I will give her her vineyards from thence, and the valley of Achor for a door of hope: and she shall sing there, as in the days of her youth, and as in the day when she came up out of the land of Egypt. And it shall be at that day, saith the LORD, that thou shalt call me Ishi; and shalt call me no more Baali. For I will take away the names of Baalim out of her mouth, and they shall no more be remembered by their name.*

*And in that day will I make a covenant for them with the beasts of the field, and with the fowls of heaven, and with the creeping things of the ground: and I will break the bow and the sword and the battle out of the earth, and will make them to lie down safely. And I will betroth thee unto me for ever; yea, I will betroth thee unto me in righteousness, and in judgment, and in lovingkindness, and in mercies. I will even betroth thee unto me in faithfulness: and thou shalt know the LORD. And it shall come to pass in that day, I will hear, saith the LORD, I will hear the heavens, and they shall hear the earth; and the earth shall hear the corn, and the wine, and the oil; and they shall hear Jezreel. And I will sow her unto me in the earth; and I will have mercy upon her that had not obtained mercy; and I will say to them which were not my people, Thou art my people; and they shall say, Thou art my God.*

This rather lengthy passage of Scripture provides the context we need for our understanding. Give special attention to an expression in verse fifteen, *"a door of hope."*

The Lord has introduced us to Hosea, Gomer, and their three children. Hosea was instructed of the Lord to marry a woman who would enter into whoredoms. She was a woman who would be unfaithful and break the covenant of marriage to go after other men. She would bear children, and the names of those children would describe her lifestyle. In the lives of Hosea, his wife, and children, God tells us the story of His relationship with Israel and her unfaithfulness to Him. He introduces us to this truth in the first chapter.

*God's children are the most hopeful people on earth.*

When we arrive at the second chapter, Hosea comes home to find that his wife is gone, though his children remain. We might imagine that we find the youngest of them weeping and the others saddened by what their mother is doing. The older children are old enough to know what their mother is engaging in and how awful this lewd, adulterous lifestyle happens to be. They are greatly troubled.

As the story unfolds in the life of this family, God wants us to look beyond the home of Hosea. He wants us to catch a glimpse of His heart and recognize His love for His people.

One of the most amazing things we discover is the pursuit of God's love. It is one of the great wonders of the Bible. Can you imagine a man with a wife like this, left at home with these children? Can you imagine a man going after her, providing for her, loving her, seeking after her, going through every den of iniquity he can find and calling out her name? He even provides for her while she is still living with her lovers so that she does not starve to death.

To those who do not love, love is insane. You cannot explain it. There is no way to bottle it up or try to describe it. With everything you can imagine and have witnessed in human love, remember that

God loves us with an everlasting love. It is a love that will never let us go. It exceeds our imagination.

Some of you may run from God and seek to hide. You may even drive God from your thoughts. You may imagine that you can go somewhere and join up with some crowd or do something to yourself or your body that drives the thought of God out of your mind. Just about the time that you think He is gone, you will turn a corner and He will be there. It is an amazing truth. This is one of the great wonders of the Bible, this pursuit of God's love. He is seeking you.

The Bible says in Hosea 2:2-4,

> *Plead with your mother, plead: for she is not my wife, neither am I her husband: let her therefore put away her whoredoms out of her sight, and her adulteries from between her breasts; lest I strip her naked, and set her as in the day that she was born, and make her as a wilderness, and set her like a dry land, and slay her with thirst. And I will not have mercy upon her children; for they be the children of whoredoms.*

We each know that sin in a family affects all of those in that family. The Bible speaks here of the effect that this sin has upon the children. God is speaking to ancient Israel about their sin and their forgetting and forsaking Him. He shows them what it is going to do to their children in the generations to come.

We need to be awakened to the truth that our lives affect the lives of our children. Our lives affect the lives of those we love. There is such selfishness in all of us. There is such self-serving and self-centeredness in all of us. We want our way, no matter how high the price or how great the consequence. God warns us that our sin affects our children (Lamentations 1:5).

I have thought so often about people with beautiful little children. I have held many of them in my arms. Many of those children, now

31

grown, are not in church; they are not listening to the preaching of the Bible. The blame for much of that has to be laid at the feet of their parents with their critical hearts and condemning attitudes. Life and death is in the power of the tongue, and so many have been slain by their own families with the tongue of some family member.

Can you imagine this man and these children left alone? The wife and mother is out there somewhere, and they know what she is doing. The Bible says in verse five, *"For their mother hath played the harlot: she that conceived them hath done shamefully: for she said, I will go after my lovers, that give me my bread and my water, my wool and my flax, mine oil and my drink."*

*Just about the time that you think He is gone, you will turn a corner, and He will be there. It is an amazing truth. This is one of the great wonders of the Bible, this pursuit of God's love. He is seeking you.*

She is gone, but Hosea has not forgotten her. Hosea will go after her. Just as surely, God has not forgotten His own, and He will go after them. He will lead them to *"a door of hope."*

The word *"therefore"* is mentioned in this chapter in verse six, verse nine, and again in verse fourteen. We are going on a journey in this second chapter to find *"a door of hope."* Where shall we find this door of hope?

*"Hope deferred maketh the heart sick: but when the desire cometh, it is a tree of life"* (Proverbs 13:12). You may get your hopes up thinking, "This is the door of hope! This is it! My loved one is coming to the Lord!" But then it does not happen, and your heart is sick. Do not give up! Our hope must be in the Lord, not in those who are away from the Lord. If you put your hope in those who are away from the Lord, you are going to stay

downhearted and disappointed; our hope must always be in God. Keep believing and trusting God.

Some of you know someone that you love dearly who is away from God. I would like to ask you this question. Is that person still alive? Is he still living? If you say yes, then listen to this verse. *"For to him that is joined to all the living there is hope: for a living dog is better than a dead lion"* (Ecclesiastes 9:4). As long as there is life, there is hope! To drive the point home, God says, "A dog that is alive is better than a dead lion." If you could choose a dog or a lion, you would choose a lion; but if you had to choose between a living dog or a dead lion, you would choose the living dog. He is illustrating to us that as long as there is life, there is hope.

# THEREFORE, A HEDGE OF THORNS

Where shall we find this door of hope? Listen as the Lord talks to us about His erring people, Israel. Again, this is illustrated in Hosea's relationship with Gomer. God Himself leads us on this path, and He marks the path often with this word *"therefore."* As we travel through the second chapter of Hosea, every time we come to the  in this progressive search, we are drawing nearer. He has given us an introduction early in chapter two, and now He brings us to the first *"therefore." "Therefore, behold, I will hedge up thy way with thorns, and make a wall, that she shall not find her paths"* (Hosea 2:6).

Can we find a door of hope among the hedges? What does God mean by this? This is a hedge of thorns. This means that God is going to place restraints on her behavior. She can only go so far. He is going to hedge her up. We often think, if our erring ones could just be brought to a certain place where they can run no further and do no more, perhaps they will find a door of hope.

The Bible says in verse seven, *"And she shall follow after her lovers, but she shall not overtake them; and she shall seek them, but shall not find them: then shall she say, I will go and return to my first husband; for then was it better with me than now."*

All of this is going on in the heart of God and in the mind of Hosea. If she is hedged up, if she can only go so far, then she is going to think, "I cannot get as far as I want to get. I cannot really pursue my lovers. I will go back to my first husband because things were better then."

She almost gets there. The thought crosses her mind, "This is no life to live! This is no way for a human being to spend his or her life! I had a home, and a husband, and children!" In like manner, an erring nation, straying from God and committing spiritual adultery, may have moments in trying times when she is hedged up by thorns. Her people cry out, "This is no way to go! We need to return to God!" But it does not happen.

Hosea has followed his wife and found someone living in a sinful relationship with her. "Are you the man that is living with Gomer? Are you the man?" The man perhaps thought, "I am about to be attacked or something worse." But Hosea says, "Are you the man?" When he finds out that the answer is yes, because he loves her and does not want her hurting, he brings to her the necessities of life, even while she is living that way.

When Gomer returns to this man Hosea found, the man lies to her and says, "Look what I have for you!" And they offer these things to a false god and forget that they came from her own husband. How low can people go? From God's vantage point, I wonder how low He thinks we have gone?

We are a people so blessed, so loved. Where do all these blessings we enjoy come from? They come from the very hand of God. We are in the worst sinful condition, yet we are still breathing the air,

drinking the water, and eating the food God provides. We continue making offerings and sacrifices to our sinful behavior and idols.

The Bible says in Job 1:9-10, *"Then Satan answered the* LORD*, and said, Doth Job fear God for nought? Hast not thou made an hedge about him, and about his house, and about all that he hath on every side? thou hast blessed the work of his hands, and his substance is increased in the land."* God placed a hedge around Job to keep the Devil out.

> *We each know that sin in a family affects all of those in that family.*

Remember, God does not hedge what is not His. But God said, "I am going to lower that hedge a bit and let you in, Devil."

The same principle is found in Hosea; the hedge is not to keep the Devil out, but to keep the sinful person from going any further to the Devil. You may think of a straying loved one and say, "I think that is what it is going to take. If God would just get him cornered off somewhere and limit what he can do, this is what it will take to bring about a door of hope." But it does not work! The very things God provides are taken and offered to the Devil.

# THEREFORE, I TAKE AWAY

So now we come to the next stepping-stone in this journey, *"therefore."* What is the Lord going to do now? Where will we find this door of hope? The Bible says in Hosea 2:9-13,

> *Therefore will I return, and take away my corn in the time thereof, and my wine in the season thereof, and will recover my wool and my flax given to cover her nakedness. And now will I discover her*

*lewdness in the sight of her lovers, and none shall deliver her out of mine hand. I will also cause all her mirth to cease, her feast days, her new moons, and her sabbaths, and all her solemn feasts. And I will destroy her vines and her fig trees, whereof she hath said, These are my rewards that my lovers have given me: and I will make them a forest, and the beasts of the field shall eat them. And I will visit upon her the days of Baalim, wherein she burned incense to them, and she decked herself with her earrings and her jewels, and she went after her lovers, and forgat me, saith the LORD.*

God says, "I am going to remove from her everything I have given to bless her. I am going to bring her to the end of herself. Nothing will be left when I get through taking away from her. First, I restrain; now, I am going to remove."

We have the idea that when people come to poverty and absolutely nothing is left, then that person will enter the door of hope. He will come to his senses now. That is what we are praying for.

Did you ever think about what will bring people to their knees? Of course, we know there is pleasure in sin for a season, but God says, "I am going to take the pleasure out of it. It is going to run its course. She has been enjoying herself, but I am going to take away everything—even the necessities."

How far has Gomer gone? The Bible says, *"She...forgat me."* First, she forsook Hosea; now she has forgotten him. Can you imagine a woman getting to the place where the thought of her husband never even comes to her mind? She has three children at home. Her three children do not even cross her mind. Not only has she forsaken them, she has forgotten them. What do people do to drive these thoughts out?

I have seen people work against their own conscience, and you have too. Maybe you have not recognized it, but you have seen someone adrift from God. They begin to say things that they never said before. As their conscience is crying out about what they ought to be doing, they begin using vile language to silence their accusing conscience. I have seen people tattoo their bodies just to say, "I am tired of this yelling and screaming on the inside! I am going to prove that I am my own boss! I will do as I please, and not even God will tell me what to do! I will drive Him out of my mind. I will forget Him! I'm not the person they think I am, and I intend to prove it." There appears to be no end to how far some will go with sin to attempt to silence an accusing conscience.

> *There appears to be no end to how far some will go with sin to attempt to silence an accusing conscience.*

God says, "I am going to deal with her. I am going to deal with Israel. I am going to take away everything that she leans on and depends on. I am going to remove every provision she has." Hosea says, "I am going to take away everything that is needed and necessary in the life of Gomer. Perhaps this will bring her back, and she will enter the door of hope." But it is so sad. She does not return. She has been hedged about, restrained, yet she does not come back. She has had things removed from her, yet she does not come back.

I know what many of you are thinking—you are thinking about your son, daughter, mother, or father. You think, "I thought surely they would have returned by now!" But they have not. As we continue down this path, we come to the third *"therefore."*

# THEREFORE,
# IN THE VALLEY OF ACHOR

Hosea 2:14-15 says, *"Therefore, behold, I will allure her, and bring her into the wilderness, and speak comfortably unto her. And I will give her her vineyards from thence, and the valley of Achor for a door of hope: and she shall sing there, as in the days of her youth, and as in the day when she came up out of the land of Egypt."*

Where do we find the door of hope? The answer is that we find *"a door of hope"* in the valley of Achor. We need to know what the valley of Achor is all about. This valley is mentioned three times in the Bible: once here, once in the book of Joshua, and once in the book of Isaiah.

*May I tell you what our problem is? We are not willing to trust God with those we love.*

In the book of Joshua, we find Joshua dealing with the city of Ai. This valley of Achor was a valley in which Achan was taken and slain. The Bible says in Joshua 7:26, *"And they raised over him a great heap of stones unto this day. So the LORD turned from the fierceness of his anger. Wherefore the name of that place was called, The valley of Achor, unto this day."* Achor means "the valley of trouble." It was a valley of trouble.

In Isaiah 65:10, we find this valley of trouble mentioned for the second time. The Bible says, *"And Sharon shall be a fold of flocks, and the valley of Achor a place for the herds to lie down in, for my people that have sought me."* God has brought the people to the valley of Achor, and now in this valley of trouble the herds are lying down. What is the Lord saying to us here?

38

Remember, we are talking about Hosea and Gomer, and God and His people; but I am dealing with our lives individually. The most unimaginable thing could take place sometime in your future. Someone you have held in your arms, prayed over, and loved could be out yonder somewhere needing to come through *"a door of hope."* Where will he find it? The Bible says that when he will not return because of being hedged in, and when he will not return because things have been taken away, God will bring him to the valley of trouble, the valley of Achor.

*It appears that your peril is unending; and then suddenly, God appears and makes a way. At that moment, when it seems you have found a point of exit, you realize it is a point of entrance. A door of hope opens to God.*

For the nation of Israel, this valley of trouble will be the Great Tribulation. Since Israel turned against God and would not receive the true Christ, their history has been a history of antichrist. The Bible even teaches us that they are going to follow the Antichrist. It will take this time of *"Jacob's trouble,"* this Great Tribulation, to bring them to their God.

The Bible says in Jeremiah 30:7, *"Alas! for that day is great, so that none is like it: it is even the time of Jacob's trouble, but he shall be saved out of it."* The world has yet to witness this most horrible time. In the darkest depth of the tribulation period, in the awful flames and furnace of that tribulation, Christ will appear–just when it looks as if Israel will be completely destroyed. They will be awakened and recognize their Messiah.

In Revelation chapters thirteen and fourteen, we see that the world will actually worship the Antichrist. Revelation 13:8 says, *"And all that dwell upon the earth shall worship him, whose names are not written in the book of life of the Lamb slain from the foundation of*

*the world."* This is not Christ that they are worshiping; this is the Antichrist. Every person whose name is not in the Lamb's Book of Life will worship the Antichrist.

If you read the thirteenth chapter of Revelation, it seems as if the whole world is in the very grasp of the Devil. All is gone; all hope is destroyed. Then you come to the fourteenth chapter and read, *"And I looked, and, lo, a Lamb stood on the mount Sion, and with him an hundred forty and four thousand, having his Father's name written in their foreheads."*

*In His hour of trouble, when He was crucified in weakness and bled and died for our sins, God opened wide a door of hope for us, through the precious work of Christ on Calvary.*

Where do we find a door of hope? We find it in this valley of trouble. May I tell you what our problem is? We are not willing to trust God with those we love. We want to see them hedged about, and we want to see things removed so that they become desperate; but we are not willing to let God take them to the valley of trouble. We do not want the Lord to go that far with those we love.

The door of hope is in the valley of trouble. In the valley of trouble, everything seems hopeless. There is no way out. For Achan, in Judges chapter seven, it was the valley of death. It was not only death for him, but death for his wife, children, and animals. It was death for every living thing associated with that man.

In the valley of Achor, this valley of trouble and death, there is no possible way out. You cannot get yourself out of that valley. There is no place else to go, and no one else to look to. No one is coming for you or coming after you. Your mom and dad are not going to be there; your husband or wife will not be there. You are all alone. It

appears that your peril is unending; and then suddenly, God appears and makes a way. At that moment, when it seems you have found a point of exit, you realize it is a point of entrance. The door of hope opens to God. Read Luke 15:11-24. We discover this is what happened to the prodigal son when he came to himself.

Read prayerfully Hosea 2:15-23 and search for the door of hope.

*And I will give her her vineyards from thence, and the valley of Achor for a door of hope: and she shall sing there, as in the days of her youth, and as in the day when she came up out of the land of Egypt. And it shall be at that day, saith the LORD, that thou shalt call me Ishi; and shalt call me no more Baali. For I will take away the names of Baalim out of her mouth, and they shall no more be remembered by their name. And in that day will I make a covenant for them with the beasts of the field, and with the fowls of heaven, and with the creeping things of the ground: and I will break the bow and the sword and the battle out of the earth, and will make them to lie down safely. And I will betroth thee unto me for ever; yea, I will betroth thee unto me in righteousness, and in judgment, and in lovingkindness, and in mercies. I will even betroth thee unto me in faithfulness: and thou shalt know the LORD. And it shall come to pass in that day, I will hear, saith the LORD, I will hear the heavens, and they shall hear the earth; and the earth shall hear the corn, and the wine, and the oil; and they shall hear Jezreel. And I will sow her unto me in the earth; and I will have mercy upon her that had not obtained mercy; and I will say to them which were not my people, Thou art my people; and they shall say, Thou art my God.*

Where did you discover the door of hope? The only place you can find it is in the valley of trouble.

The Lord Jesus said in John 12:27, *"Now is my soul troubled; and what shall I say? Father, save me from this hour: but for this cause came I unto this hour."* Where did we find our hope? In His hour of trouble, when He was crucified in weakness and bled and died for our sins, God opened wide a door of hope for us, through the precious work of Christ on Calvary, through His death, burial, and resurrection.

Beloved, there is hope in the Lord! Commit your loved ones to Him; commit your way to Him; commit all to God. Pray that others will find this door of hope. The door of hope that we have found is in the valley of trouble. This door opens by the mercy of God into His loving presence.

# CHAPTER THREE

# GOD'S
# REDEEMING LOVE

e cannot fully comprehend the love of God. His love for sinners is not based on our behavior or beauty. He loves us in spite of our sin. The message of His redeeming love is the heart and core of the gospel.

God sent Hosea after Gomer. Hosea obeyed the Lord's command. Dear friend, it is the love of Christ that constrains us to go after the lost. Hosea 3:1- 5 says,

> Then said the LORD unto me, Go yet, love a woman beloved of her friend, yet an adulteress, according to the love of the LORD toward the children of Israel, who look to other gods, and love flagons of wine. So I bought her to me for fifteen pieces of silver, and for an homer of barley, and an half homer of barley: and I said unto her, Thou shalt abide for me many days; thou shalt not play the harlot, and thou shalt not be for another man: so will I also be for thee. For the children of Israel shall abide many days without a king, and without a prince, and without a sacrifice,

*and without an image, and without an ephod, and without teraphim: afterward shall the children of Israel return, and seek the LORD their God, and David their king; and shall fear the LORD and his goodness in the latter days.*

God's Word declares in verse two, *"So I bought her."* This is the message of God's redeeming love.

Hosea had taken a wife of whoredoms. She left him and her children. As a matter of fact, it was doubtful as to whether or not her second child actually belonged to Hosea, and we are absolutely sure that the third child was not his. She had literally gone into the depths of sin.

Perhaps at one time she was a beautiful woman, a woman whose company was desired by many people; but her life has been devastated by her sin. Sin always takes its terrible toll. There is pleasure in sin for a season, but the season is soon ended and nothing is left but death.

# THE GOD WHO SEEKS

Hosea 3:1 says, *"Then said the LORD unto me, Go yet, love a woman beloved of her friend, yet an adulteress, according to the love of the LORD toward the children of Israel, who look to other gods, and love flagons of wine."* Our God is a seeking God. Remember, God is using this marriage to illustrate His relationship with His people. God has a wife, and that wife is Israel, and of course she is to be faithful to Him.

If you recall your wedding, someone perhaps stood before you and asked, "Will you take this person to be your wedded husband or wife….Will you love and be faithful, honor and keep…?" You made a vow to love and cherish till death. No doubt, these two were reminded of the covenant that they made. Gomer broke it, and Israel had broken it with God. We learn in this passage that our God is the God who seeks. You cannot escape Him.

The Bible says in Luke 19:10, *"For the Son of man is come to seek and to save that which was lost."* Our hearts should rejoice to know that He is seeking. In the fifteenth chapter of Luke, as sinners gathered around the Saviour, He told a parable that unfolds in three stories. He told of a man with one hundred sheep;

> *Our God is the God who seeks. You cannot escape Him.*

one was lost and he sought that sheep. He spoke of a woman with ten coins; one coin was lost, and she sought that coin. He told of a man with two sons; one was gone, and he sought after that son. Our God is the God who seeks.

The attitude of most people is, "He is finished. It is over. He is worthless and useless. Nothing but a useless piece of flesh is left. No one would love him or care about him." But God is still seeking the most debased, wretched, and vile human being. He is the God who seeks. Hosea never stopped seeking his wife.

# THE GOD WHO SUFFERS

Let us understand something about the heart of God. Luke 23:27-28 says, *"And there followed him a great company of people, and of women, which also bewailed and lamented him. But Jesus turning unto them said, Daughters of Jerusalem, weep not for me, but weep for yourselves, and for your children."* When we do Him wrong, we are harming ourselves.

Do you believe that Gomer was hurting herself? I think all of us know that. When we are thinking properly, we all understand that when a person is moving away from God, that person is hurting himself.

Do you think the heart of Hosea was hurting? Why? Was it hurting from rejection? In one sense, love is the sum of all God's attributes. Everything we attribute to God is summed up in His love. He loves us with an everlasting love. He suffers with us. He will not tolerate sin, but when we are hurting, He is hurting.

In the rearing of our two sons, from time to time my wife and I have had conversations about them that went like this: "We are not hurting because they are not doing what we want them to do; we are not hurting because we feel rejected; we are hurting because they are hurting." When you truly love someone, and he is hurting, you hurt with him.

In Luke 19:41-44, our Lord stood over Jerusalem and wept. He poured out His heart over a lost, sinful people and spoke of how He would have gathered them. I believe that as Hosea is seeking after his wife Gomer and as he recognizes the hurt she has brought to herself, he too suffers with her. I am convinced that God is a God who suffers. His heart bleeds. He feels. He cares.

# THE GOD WHO SAVES

Try to imagine Hosea arriving at a slave market. We know quite a bit about ancient slave markets because so much has been written about slavery. In the ancient world, someone could become a slave by one of three ways. Some people became slaves by conquest. After a battle was lost, the defeated people would be enslaved to the victors. Others became slaves by being born to a slave. A person could also become a slave by being indebted.

Here is a woman who has spent all. She has nothing. What beauty she may have had is now vanished. What possessions she may have had are all gone. Even while she was in sin, her husband provided certain necessities for her. He later went to retrieve those things at God's bidding. Remember, even while we are sinning, we are still enjoying God's air and the health, strength, and freedom that God gives us. We are still enjoying so many of God's blessings while we are running so far away from Him.

When Hosea found Gomer, he found her at a slave market. Remember, the Lord Jesus on His way to the cross said in His comments to those women, *"Weep for yourselves."* They were hurting themselves because they were rejecting Him. We hurt ourselves as we reject the Lord.

This heartbroken husband purchased his own wife out of slavery. The Bible says in Hosea 3:2, *"So I bought her to me for fifteen pieces of silver, and for an homer of barley, and an half homer of barley."* Hosea watched his wife go on the stand to be auctioned as a slave. We are told that when slaves were sold, all their clothing was taken off. I want to deal with this as discreetly as possible, but there is nothing before us but this visual image of naked flesh standing with no possession. We look upon what sin has wrought.

*Everything we attribute to God is summed up in His love. He loves us with an everlasting love. He suffers with us. He will not tolerate sin, but when we are hurting, He is hurting.*

The bidding started. This was not some ordinary woman standing there. This was a woman who had born three children and was the wife of Hosea. Oh, dear friend, the Lord would have us see that this is not any ordinary person! This is His cherished Israel that He loves with an everlasting love! They have forsaken their God and have gone after other lovers. Sin has taken them farther into the depths of horror than they ever imagined.

The bidding does not move quickly or go very high, because there is not much left of this sinful woman. As those gazing on look at her, they find little to be desired. Yet there is someone who loves her more deeply than words can describe. A cry from the crowd says, "Twelve!"

"Thirteen pieces of silver!"

"Fourteen pieces of silver!"

Every time someone bids, someone else bids higher. There is a man in the crowd who is determined to pay whatever it costs to get her.

We are told that fifteen pieces of silver is only half of what a slave would be worth. Evidently, she was so far gone that no one else would pay more. So for Gomer on that auction block, stripped of everything, Hosea bid fifteen pieces of silver, an homer of barley, and a half homer of barley. He bought her. He redeemed her from slavery.

The bidding is over, and the Bible says in Hosea 3:3-4,

> *And I said unto her, Thou shalt abide for me many days; thou shalt not play the harlot, and thou shalt not be for another man: so will I also be for thee. For the children of Israel shall abide many days without a king, and without a prince, and without a sacrifice, and without an image, and without an ephod, and without teraphim.*

God applies all of this to Israel, and He tells us the things that they will be without. They have been people with a king, with a prince, with a sacrifice, with images, ephods, and teraphims; now they will not have them. This *"teraphim"* is evidently an idolatrous means of divination. The ephod we know to be what the high priest wore with the names of the tribes of Israel inscribed on it. He said, "You are going to be without these things."

He said further in verse five, *"Afterward shall the children of Israel return, and seek the LORD their God, and David their king; and shall fear the LORD and his goodness in the latter days."* Notice that little word *"afterward."* Praise God that there is an afterward!

50

He says, "Your life has been wrecked and ruined; you have been sold as a slave on an auction block for half the price of a slave because you have stooped so low and gone so far. To everyone else, you are worthless; but I have redeemed you! I want to bring you in quietly with me." He is speaking now of the restoration of Israel and what is going to happen to them afterward. We must understand that God has an *"afterward"* for His people!

For all of God's children, for all those the Lord seeks, He knows that there is something in the future. The Devil says, "You have sinned; you are ruined and wrecked. It is all over and you will amount to nothing." But God comes seeking after you to bring you to Himself. There is an afterward! There is a time of restoration!

We will not love the Lord like we ought to love Him or serve the Lord like we ought to serve Him until we see ourselves standing on that auction block where Gomer stood. That is not just Hosea's wife. That is you! That is me! We have been redeemed by the blood of the Lamb!

The Devil is a liar. Everything he says is a lie. He even mixes some so-called "half-truths" with his lies, but it is all lies and deceit. He may tell you that he wants you, that you are needed and necessary. He may tell you that he will make you happy. But when he is finished with you, you will be left in nakedness to be sold to the highest bidder. The world looks on and decides you are not worth nearly what you might imagine.

> *We will not love the Lord like we ought to love Him or serve the Lord like we ought to serve Him until we see ourselves standing on that auction block where Gomer stood. That is not just Hosea's wife. That is you! That is me! We have been redeemed by the blood of the Lamb!*

Standing there is a Bidder. He is Someone who cares and loves with an everlasting love. He pays the price for redemption. As a matter of fact, that word *redeemed* is a word that was used in the slave markets. It is a word that grows out of this experience and describes what was done for Gomer that day.

*Some have not gone into the far country by leaving home; they have gone into the far country while staying in the church services and allowing their hearts to grow cold and indifferent.*

The Lord says in I Corinthians 6:19-20, *"What? know ye not that your body is the temple of the Holy Ghost which is in you, which ye have of God, and ye are not your own? For ye are bought with a price: therefore glorify God in your body, and in your spirit, which are God's."* Once we understand this, we see ourselves as we truly are: stripped of everything and standing on that auction block with nothing but the howling wolves of hell to take our lives to greater wreck and ruin.

I recognize that I owe a debt I cannot pay. Oh praise God, He broke through and bought me for Himself, loved me, and came to me to save and redeem me! Now I owe a debt, a debt of love and gratitude to God for sending His only begotten Son, who bled and died for my sins, who was buried and rose from the dead. I Peter 1:18-19 says, *"Forasmuch as ye know that ye were not redeemed with corruptible things, as silver and gold, from your vain conversation received by tradition from your fathers; but with the precious blood of Christ, as of a lamb without blemish and without spot."*

Gomer had lived the life of a harlot, cast out and unwanted. She was a slave to sin. Sin says, "You can do as you please!" But before long, sin becomes the master, and you become the slave to sin.

In Hosea 2:16 God says, *"Thou shalt call me Ishi; and shalt call me no more Baali."* **Baali** means "my master." This speaks of a man with a mistress. God says, "You are going to call me *Ishi*," which means "husband." The Lord is saying, "You have been a mistress to a master. You are going to return and be a wife to a husband."

Some have not gone into the far country by leaving home; they have gone into the far country while staying in the church services and allowing their hearts to grow cold and indifferent.

We are never going to do what is right until we see ourselves stripped of everything, standing on that auction block, waiting for someone to purchase us. When a person has been there and seen himself that way, he does not have to be begged to serve God.

The auctioneer says, "What will be the bid?"

The Lord Jesus says, "I will pay my precious blood."

"What? For this worthless piece of flesh? This spent and ruined human being?"

"Yes, I will pay my precious blood. I will come to a sin-cursed earth, live a reproached life, and be mocked and spat upon. I will go to Calvary and pour out my life to pay the price of redemption with my own blood for that lost soul."

That He did. He paid it all! When He saves you from sin and you recognize what it cost Him, you will have a love and devotion for Him. We love him because He first loved us.

When I get weary in well doing, I think, "What is the cure?" The cure is Calvary. With a fresh glimpse of the Son of God, I remember myself on that auction block, and I recognize that He is the God who sought me. He is the God who suffers with me. He is the God who saved me!

CHAPTER FOUR

# EPHRAIM IS JOINED TO IDOLS

he stage has been set for the remainder of the book of Hosea. The message grows out of the love story we have witnessed in chapters one through three. We have been dealing with the home of Hosea, Gomer, and their children. What the Lord has allowed us to see illustrated in their family life is a reflection upon a sinning and erring nation.

When we come to the fourth chapter, the Lord takes us directly into the homeland of Israel and shows us what was going on to provide the justification for His judgment upon His people.

Hosea 4:1-19 say,

> *Hear the word of the LORD, ye children of Israel: for the LORD hath a controversy with the inhabitants of the land, because there is no truth, nor mercy, nor knowledge of God in the land. By swearing, and lying, and killing, and stealing, and committing adultery, they break out, and blood toucheth blood.*

*Therefore shall the land mourn, and every one that dwelleth therein shall languish, with the beasts of the field, and with the fowls of heaven; yea, the fishes of the sea also shall be taken away. Yet let no man strive, nor reprove another: for thy people are as they that strive with the priest. Therefore shalt thou fall in the day, and the prophet also shall fall with thee in the night, and I will destroy thy mother.*

*My people are destroyed for lack of knowledge: because thou hast rejected knowledge, I will also reject thee, that thou shalt be no priest to me: seeing thou hast forgotten the law of thy God, I will also forget thy children. As they were increased, so they sinned against me: therefore will I change their glory into shame. They eat up the sin of my people, and they set their heart on their iniquity. And there shall be, like people, like priest: and I will punish them for their ways, and reward them their doings. For they shall eat, and not have enough: they shall commit whoredom, and shall not increase: because they have left off to take heed to the LORD.*

*Whoredom and wine and new wine take away the heart. My people ask counsel at their stocks, and their staff declareth unto them: for the spirit of whoredoms hath caused them to err, and they have gone a whoring from under their God. They sacrifice upon the tops of the mountains, and burn incense upon the hills, under oaks and poplars and elms, because the shadow thereof is good: therefore your daughters shall commit whoredom, and your spouses shall commit adultery. I will not punish your daughters when they commit whoredom, nor your spouses when they commit adultery: for themselves are separated with whores, and they sacrifice with harlots: therefore the people that doth not understand shall fall. Though thou, Israel, play the harlot, yet let not Judah offend; and come not ye unto Gilgal, neither go ye up to Bethaven, nor swear, The LORD liveth.*

*For Israel slideth back as a backsliding heifer: now the LORD will feed them as a lamb in a large place. Ephraim is joined to idols: let him alone. Their drink is sour: they have committed whoredom continually: her rulers with shame do love, Give ye. The wind hath bound her up in her wings, and they shall be ashamed because of their sacrifices.*

Ephraim is the dominant tribe in the northern kingdom. When God says, *"Ephraim is joined to idols: let him alone,"* He is speaking to Judah. After the reign of Solomon, the kingdom of Israel divided into the northern kingdom and the southern kingdom.

In the northern kingdom, the people were led to two places of worship. Of all things, golden calves were erected in a place called Beth-el and a place called Gilgal. They were told in the beginning that these golden calves only represented the Lord, because the location of the temple and Jerusalem was in the southern kingdom.

*Immorality is always preceded by idolatry. When something or someone takes the place of God, it is going to affect the behavior of that person.*

So in the northern kingdom, they assigned these places as places of worship. God had warned them not to have these images. The

57

things that were to represent God became their gods. Now the Lord, through the prophet Hosea, speaks to the nation of Israel.

In the middle of his preaching in the fourth chapter, he proclaims this to Judah, "Ephraim (meaning Israel) is joined unto idols. They are worshiping images." God says, *"Let him alone."*

> *Because we have so much information, we may think that we have the truth. Does the Lord find truth in our land? The only worth-while thing we can pass from one generation to the next is truth.*

We are going through this chapter, but I want to give you a principle that will help you all of your life. Once you understand this principle, you will understand something about the behavior of people. Once you understand this principle, you will remember first what caused their behavior when seeking to change it. No matter how hard you try to change their behavior, unless something is done to change the heart, the behavior will never be changed.

The principle is that *immorality* is always preceded by *idolatry.* When something or someone takes the place of God, it is going to affect the behavior of that person. When you see what is going wrong in the life of a person, when you witness immoral behavior and see actions that you know are not right, remember that those actions were caused by that person not giving God His rightful place in his life.

Not only do we see this in the lives of individuals, we also witness this in the life of ancient Israel and in the life of our own nation. Often people ask, "What has gone wrong in America?" When I was a school child years ago, people talked about the big problems in schools being chewing gum in class, throwing paper wads, and sticking nasty things on the ceiling. I cannot remember one person in my high school that used drugs. I only heard about drugs once. It just did not happen. Some people were drinking alcohol, but I just did not hear of drugs. We had one place where people who smoked would go to smoke during school breaks. I never went there, and I did not have many friends who went back there; but I do not ever remember any young lady going back there with those boys. It just did not happen.

We have gone through a great drift in the moral behavior of our nation. Does anyone ever wonder how this happened? When we do away with the true and living God, every type of behavior imaginable becomes permissible.

As we travel back to Hosea chapter four, we are dealing with events that happened nearly 2700 years ago, but we find the very same principle applies to today. Hosea 4:17 says, *"Ephraim is joined to idols: let him alone."*

# THE WITNESS GOD GIVES CONCERNING THE LAND

This fourth chapter serves as an introduction for the rest of the book. This is what God says is wrong in the land. If we are given the opportunity, we might say something else, but this is what God says brought about judgment. We ought to give serious heed to this, because the Lord is going right to the source. God Himself takes the witness stand.

Hosea 4:1 says, *"Hear the word of the LORD, ye children of Israel: for the LORD hath a controversy with the inhabitants of the land..."* Why should God even mention the land? Because He gave them that land. He delivered them from bondage and brought them into this land. Now He declares, *"...the LORD hath a controversy with the inhabitants of the land, because there is no truth, nor mercy, nor knowledge of God in the land."* The root of it all is that there is no truth in the land.

I am sure you have heard many people say that we live in an information age. When I was just a boy and computers were being introduced, there were only certain "wizards" who could operate a computer, and these computers were multi-thousand dollar machines. A genius of some kind was the only person within hundreds of miles who could operate one. It was a powerful machine! If you saw one of them, it was something large enough to fill an entire room! We have come a long way in our ability to access information.

Because we have so much information, we may think that we have the truth. Does the Lord find truth in our land? The only worthwhile thing we can pass from one generation to the next is truth.

Because there is no *"truth,"* there is no *"mercy."* What has brought about the hardening of a generation? What has brought on abusive families? What has brought on this lack of courtesy and kindness? We have no truth and therefore, have no mercy.

The third thing that God says is that there is no *"knowledge of God"* in the land. We have become a garden of strange gods, but there is so little knowledge of the only true God—the Creator of heaven and earth.

We read in Proverbs 3:1-4,

> *My son, forget not my law; but let thine heart keep my commandments: for length of days, and long life, and peace, shall they add to thee. Let not mercy and truth forsake thee: bind them about thy neck; write them upon the table of thine heart: so shalt thou find favour and good understanding in the sight of God and man.*

In other words, if you are going to hold on to anything, make sure you hold on to mercy and truth! God warns of a certain generation.

We read in Proverbs 30:11-14,

> *There is a generation that curseth their father, and doth not bless their mother. There is a generation that are pure in their own eyes, and yet is not washed from their filthiness. There is a generation, O how lofty are their eyes! and their eyelids are lifted up. There is a generation, whose teeth are as swords, and their jaw teeth as knives, to devour the poor from off the earth, and the needy from among men.*

We live in a very frightening age. We live when people are extremely afraid. Children are scared to go into a public restroom alone. People are scared to walk out of their houses at night. People are scared to drive through an unfamiliar area. They are frightened everywhere because they know that people have become cruel and without mercy.

How did this happen? It happened when we became a nation of idolaters. We have dethroned God! Idolatry always precedes immorality.

We see where this leads as God continues to witness. Verse two says, *"By swearing, and lying, and killing, and stealing, and committing adultery, they break out, and blood toucheth blood."* The expression *"blood toucheth blood"* means that it is continual. One crime runs into another crime.

Everything in the land is affected adversely because of sin. God says in verse three, *"Therefore shall the land*

*We have become a garden of strange gods, but there is so little knowledge of the only true God— the Creator of heaven and earth.*

*mourn, and every one that dwelleth therein shall languish, with the beasts of the field, and with the fowls of heaven; yea, the fishes of the sea also shall be taken away."*

# THE WICKEDNESS OF THE PEOPLE

At whom does the Lord point His finger? God singles out the priests, those who should be leaders. Hosea 4:4 says, *"Yet let no man strive, nor reprove another: for thy people are as they that strive with the priest."*

In Deuteronomy 17:8-13, God established a principle about how things were to be dealt with. He said,

> *If there arise a matter too hard for thee in judgment, between blood and blood, between plea and plea, and between stroke and stroke, being matters of controversy within thy gates: then shalt thou arise, and get thee up into the place which the LORD thy God shall choose; and thou shalt come unto the priests the Levites, and unto the judge that shall be in those days, and enquire; and they shall shew thee the sentence of judgment: and thou shalt do according to the sentence, which they of that place which the LORD shall choose shall shew thee; and thou shalt observe to do according to all that they inform thee: according to the sentence of the law which they shall teach thee, and according to the judgment which they shall tell thee, thou shalt do: thou shalt not decline from the sentence which they shall shew thee, to the right hand, nor to the left. And the man that will do presumptuously, and will not hearken unto the priest that standeth to minister there before the LORD thy God, or unto the judge, even that man shall die: and thou shalt put away the evil from*

*Israel. And all the people shall hear, and fear, and do no more presumptuously.*

The Lord gave very clear instructions concerning controversy and how it should be handled. The Lord's counsel went unheeded.

According to what God says in Hosea 4:4, corruption became the order of the day. A nation of idolaters lived in a land filled with immorality.

Hosea 4:5 says, *"Therefore shalt thou fall in the day, and the prophet also shall fall with thee in the night, and I will destroy thy mother."* I cannot imagine the most blessed people on the face of the earth being spoken of this way. Think of all that God did to bring into existence the nation of Israel. God is going to restore them someday, but for now He is going to use the Assyrians to take into captivity the nation of Israel. He goes so far as to say, *"I will destroy thy mother."* This idolatrous behavior must be stopped.

There are those who say that this could never happen to America. Even some of our great leaders of long ago said, "If this nation ever does fall, it will not be because of some mighty strength on the outside; it will be because of decay and rottenness on the inside." How does it happen? It is connected to the place that we give to God.

The verdict of the Almighty continues in Hosea 4:6, *"My people are destroyed for lack of knowledge: because thou hast rejected knowledge, I will also reject thee, that thou shalt be no priest to me: seeing thou hast forgotten the law of thy God, I will also forget thy children."*

The children will be forgotten. Think of how our actions affect the next generation. Parents, what about your children? My wife and I decided long ago that so much of what we do is not for us, but for our children and grandchildren.

The Lord continues in verse seven, *"As they were increased, so they sinned against me: therefore will I change their glory into shame."*

Israel was once the glory of all the earth. Now the glory is changed to shame. Could this happen to our beloved America? Unless America returns to God, it not only can happen, but it will happen.

The priests face further judgment in verse eight, *"They eat up the sin of my people, and they set their heart on their iniquity."* The leaders live on the sin of the people. They have entered into it themselves, and they gain from it.

Verse nine tells us there is no difference between the sinful behavior of the priest and the people. *"And there shall be, like people, like priest: and I will punish them for their ways, and reward them their doings."* The Lord says, *"like people, like priest."*

If you are going to lead, it will cost you something. I personally do not believe that I have ever given up anything for Jesus Christ compared to His great sacrifice on Calvary. It costs something to lead as a mother, a father, a pastor or a teacher. There must be abandonment to following God in order to be the example that God wants us to be. The Christian life is a holy life; search your Bible and you will not find it to be anything else.

I know what people say about churches like the one I pastor. Many say that we take it all too seriously. My friend, the world is on fire! Children are perishing. We live in a land where children have no faith. The situation is desperate, but so many of God's people are not desperate.

Verse ten continues, *"For they shall eat, and not have enough: they shall commit whoredom, and shall not increase: because they have left off to take heed to the LORD."* Sin is never enough. The sinner is never satisfied.

Verse eleven and twelve say, *"Whoredom and wine and new wine take away the heart. My people ask counsel at their stocks, and their staff declareth unto them."*

Where are people looking for counsel and advice today? I read recently that 70 million Americans read their horoscopes every day. In a study conducted by Sue Blackmore and Marianne Seebold among students in England, every student surveyed knew their star sign.

Verse twelve goes on to say, *"...for the spirit of whoredoms hath caused them to err, and they have gone a whoring from under their God."* This is a spiritual warfare. God says that there is actually a spirit from the Devil that seduces to whoredoms. Do you realize that you are in a spiritual battle? Thank God, *"Greater is he that is in you, than he that is in the world"* (I John 4:4).

Hosea 4:13 says, *"They sacrifice upon the tops of the mountains, and burn incense upon the hills, under oaks and poplars and elms, because the shadow thereof is good: therefore your daughters shall commit whoredom, and your spouses shall commit adultery."* Can you imagine a people who once worshiped the true and living God now out under every

*The situation is desperate, but so many of God's people are not desperate.*

tree having their own worship service with some graven image? Have you heard about people with things in their home that they look to for strength and help? We have become a garden of gods in America.

God says in verse fourteen, *"I will not punish your daughters when they commit whoredom, nor your spouses when they commit adultery: for themselves are separated with whores, and they sacrifice with harlots: therefore the people that doth not understand shall fall."* God says, "I am not going to deal with them anymore. I am not going to discipline them anymore. I have given them over to their ways."

This is truly amazing. God says, *"I will not punish your daughters."* Then He says in verse fifteen, *"Though thou, Israel, play the harlot, yet let not Judah offend; and come not ye unto Gilgal, neither go ye up to Bethaven, nor swear, The LORD liveth."*

# THE WARNING GIVEN TO JUDAH

The Lord warned Judah to stay away from Israel. He said, *"Ephraim is joined to idols: let him alone."* Remember the use of the word *Ephraim* is a term used collectively for Israel.

*We need to guard our hearts from being joined to idols and make sure that we keep God on the throne of our lives.*

We read in verse sixteen, *"For Israel slideth back as a backsliding heifer: now the LORD will feed them as a lamb in a large place."* He tells us what He is going to do to Israel. He explains, "I am going to let them loose in a large place like a lamb, lost, bleating, and crying out for help. This will not be a confined place. I will put this lonely lamb in the middle of a large place." Because they want their freedom, they are going to be delivered to the Assyrians and then scattered throughout the nations.

Do you want your freedom? Do you want to do as you please and have your way? God says, "I am going to remove you from the land and put you as a lamb in a large place, and you are going to find out that it is not what you wanted after all."

You and I need to heed this warning, friends. Do not ever think this cannot happen to you. Better men than the man writing these words to you have fallen. Better churches than ours have been disrupted and nearly destroyed. Better homes than the one you and I have, have been ripped apart. We need to guard our hearts from being joined to idols and make sure that we keep God on the throne of our lives.

Hosea 4:18-19 says, *"Their drink is sour: they have committed whoredom continually: her rulers with shame do love, Give ye. The wind hath bound her up in her wings, and they shall be ashamed because of their sacrifices."* There is coming a reckoning day when every man will stand before God. Every knee is going to bow and every tongue will confess that Jesus Christ is Lord. That is going to happen because the Bible says it is going to happen (Philippians 2:9-11).

The witness God gave concerning the land of His people—no truth, no mercy, and no knowledge of God—I believe is the same witness God gives of our land. The people dethroned God in their lives and lived wickedly. That principle is always connected. The place we give God determines the place that we give everything else.

If you are going to have conflict with your children, and you certainly will as you attempt to rear them, you need to understand something that is extremely important. When you are trying to change their behavior, and it is impossible to get them to do what is right, you ought to pray more earnestly that they would give God His rightful place in their lives. Then they will have a heart to do what is right.

The warning God gives to Judah is the one we must heed. What happened to Israel could also happen to Judah, and eventually it did. What has happened in the lives of many people who have fallen could also happen to us if we do not keep the Lord in His rightful place on a daily basis. Your sons and daughters could go down just like you have seen other sons and daughters go down. Your husband or wife could fall just as you have witnessed others fall. This ought to cause us to fear the Lord, to love Him, serve Him, and to keep Him as the God of our lives. Ephraim is joined to idols!

## Chapter Five

# In Their Affliction Will They Seek Me Early

 he history of the world is a history of hurt. The hope of the human heart finds fulfillment only in the Lord. Affliction can be a tool used of God to bring people to Himself. The record of the human race proves that people are more open to the message of Jesus Christ during affliction. Hosea 5:1-15 says,

*Hear ye this, O priests; and hearken, ye house of Israel; and give ye ear, O house of the king; for judgment is toward you, because ye have been a snare on Mizpah, and a net spread upon Tabor. And the revolters are profound to make slaughter, though I have been a rebuker of them all. I know Ephraim, and Israel is not hid from me: for now, O Ephraim, thou committest whoredom, and Israel is defiled. They will not frame their doings to turn unto their God: for the spirit of whoredoms is in the midst of them, and they have not known the LORD. And the pride of Israel doth testify to his face: therefore shall*

*Israel and Ephraim fall in their iniquity; Judah also shall fall with them.*

*They shall go with their flocks and with their herds to seek the LORD; but they shall not find him; he hath withdrawn himself from them. They have dealt treacherously against the LORD: for they have begotten strange children: now shall a month devour them with their portions. Blow ye the cornet in Gibeah, and the trumpet in Ramah: cry aloud at Bethaven, after thee, O Benjamin. Ephraim shall be desolate in the day of rebuke: among the tribes of Israel have I made known that which shall surely be. The princes of Judah were like them that remove the bound: therefore I will pour out my wrath upon them like water. Ephraim is oppressed and broken in judgment, because he willingly walked after the commandment. Therefore will I be unto Ephraim as a moth, and to the house of Judah as rottenness.*

*When Ephraim saw his sickness, and Judah saw his wound, then went Ephraim to the Assyrian, and sent to king Jareb: yet could he not heal you, nor cure you of your wound. For I will be unto Ephraim as a lion, and as a young lion to the house of Judah: I, even I, will tear and go away; I will take away, and none shall rescue him. I will go and return to my place, till they acknowledge their offence, and seek my face: in their affliction they will seek me early.*

God says of His people in the closing part of verse fifteen, *"In their affliction they will seek me early."* The Bible teaches us that the goodness of God leads us to repentance (Romans 2:4). That is the way it should always be. We should respond to the Lord because of

His goodness to us. Here the Bible says that God must bring affliction on the people, and because of that affliction, they will seek the Lord.

The Bible says in Psalms 119:67-71,

> *Before I was afflicted I went astray: but now have I kept thy word. Thou art good, and doest good; teach me thy statutes. The proud have forged a lie against me: but I will keep thy precepts with my whole heart. Their heart is as fat as grease; but I delight in thy law. It is good for me that I have been afflicted; that I might learn thy statutes.*

The psalmist acknowledges that it has taken the affliction God brought on his life to *"learn thy statues."* Affliction was used to bring him to the place where he recognized God's statutes and was willing to be obedient to the Lord.

As we come back to the beginning of Hosea five we read, *"Hear ye this, O priests; and hearken, ye house of Israel; and give ye ear, O house of the king."* He says to the priest and the king, "I have a message for you." He says,

> *Judgment is toward you, because ye have been a snare on Mizpah, and a net spread upon Tabor. And the revolters are profound to make slaughter, though I have been a rebuker of them all. I know Ephraim, and Israel is not hid from me: for now, O Ephraim, thou committest whoredom, and Israel is defiled.*

He says, *"I know Ephraim."* People get the idea that God does not keep up with everything—only the big things we do. The Lord is declaring here that all things are known to Him. The Lord says, *"I know."* He knows our thoughts. He knows all about us. He not only knows what we do, but He knows the cause and motive behind what we do.

71

Hosea 5:4 says, *"They will not frame their doings to turn unto their God: for the spirit of whoredoms is in the midst of them, and they have not known the LORD."* This *"spirit of whoredoms"* is an indication that this is not simply a battle of flesh and blood. No doubt, in the closing hours of the nation of Israel, the Devil intensified his effort, before they were led away into captivity by the Assyrians, and *"the spirit of whoredoms"* came upon the land. We need to be wide-awake and aware that we are in a spiritual conflict. *"For we wrestle not against flesh and blood, but against principalities, against powers, against the rulers of the darkness of this world, against spiritual wickedness in high places"* (Ephesians 6:12).

> *The old nature spends its entire existence attempting to figure out how we can live without God.*

Hosea 5:5 continues, *"And the pride of Israel doth testify to his face: therefore shall Israel and Ephraim fall in their iniquity; Judah also shall fall with them."* The *"pride"* of the people brought them to destruction. Pride subtly works on all of us to live our lives without dependence upon God. As a matter of fact, the old nature spends its entire existence attempting to figure out how we can live without God.

It is shocking to read in verse six that God is gone. *"They shall go with their flocks and with their herds to seek the LORD; but they shall not find him; he hath withdrawn himself from them."*

Then we read in verses seven and eight, *"They have dealt treacherously against the LORD: for they have begotten strange children: now shall a month devour them with their portions. Blow ye the cornet in Gibeah, and the trumpet in Ramah: cry aloud at Bethaven, after thee, O Benjamin."* The cornet was sounded to warn of the enemy's coming. "The enemy is at the door! Blow the cornet!"

The trumpet was most often used in worship. "Sound the trumpet indicating you need the Lord! Go ahead. Cry aloud at Bethaven." *Bethaven* means "the house of emptiness." In contrast, *Beth-el* is "the house of God." God says, "You cry aloud but it is too late. It is a house of emptiness."

God says in verses nine and ten, *"Ephraim shall be desolate in the day of rebuke: among the tribes of Israel have I made known that which shall surely be. The princes of Judah were like them that remove the bound: therefore I will pour out my wrath upon them like water."* When God gave the land to the people, they established landmarks, and they were not to remove those ancient landmarks. From generation to generation, they were to keep those landmarks, those boundaries. When God gave them a certain portion, there were boundaries that defined their portion. God said, "You have foolishly removed all the boundaries." The Lord has given us boundaries for our own protection.

God's people have done away with most boundaries. We do as we please, not as the Lord pleases. We compare ourselves with the world and the worldlings. We find someone doing much worse than we are doing, and we judge by their behavior that we are doing better than most people. God holds a different standard for His people because of the light He has given them.

The Lord Jesus established His headquarters for His earthly ministry in a place called Capernaum. Do you know what He said about Capernaum? *"And thou, Capernaum, which art exalted unto heaven, shalt be brought down to hell: for if the mighty works, which have been done in thee, had been done in Sodom, it would have remained until this day"* (Matthew 11:23). Today it is a desolate place.

The Lord Jesus never preached in Sodom and Gomorrah. The truth of God's Word was never proclaimed in those evil cities. We sin against such light! Even in America, we compare ourselves with other nations. The people of other nations have not had the light we have had! Did you ever think about what light we are sinning against?

73

I think about this perhaps as much as any other thing in my life. As I consider how good God has been to me, and how much He has revealed to me, and how much opportunity I have been given, I think of how accountable I am to God. The Lord places boundaries on our lives for our good because He loves us. He says, "Because these people did away with the boundaries," the Lord says, *"therefore I will pour out my wrath upon them like water."*

God declares in verse eleven, *"Ephraim is oppressed and broken in judgment, because he willingly walked after the commandment."* Notice that little word *"commandment."* Remember, when the kingdom was divided, Rehoboam and Jeroboam took their respective places; Rehoboam in the south and Jeroboam in the north. In I Kings 12:25-28, Jeroboam gave a commandment. The Bible says,

> *Then Jeroboam built Shechem in mount Ephraim, and dwelt therein; and went out from thence, and built Penuel. And Jeroboam said in his heart, Now shall the kingdom return to the house of David: if this people go up to do sacrifice in the house of the LORD at Jerusalem, then shall the heart of this people turn again unto their lord, even unto Rehoboam king of Judah, and they shall kill me, and go again to Rehoboam king of Judah. Whereupon the king took counsel, and made two calves of gold, and said unto them, It is too much for you to go up to Jerusalem: behold thy gods, O Israel, which brought thee up out of the land of Egypt.*

This man said to Israel, "It is too much for you to go all the way to Jerusalem. I made these two calves. Behold, these are your gods! Do you want to worship? You do not need to be inconvenienced. You do not need to sacrifice and go to Jerusalem!" Their leader instructed them not to be encumbered. The Bible goes on in verses twenty-nine to thirty-three,

*And he set the one in Beth-el, and the other put he in Dan. And this thing became a sin: for the people went to worship before the one, even unto Dan. And he made an house of high places, and made priests of the lowest of the people, which were not of the sons of Levi. And Jeroboam ordained a feast in the eighth month, on the fifteenth day of the month, like unto the feast that is in Judah, and he offered upon the altar. So did he in Beth-el, sacrificing unto the calves that he had made: and he placed in Beth-el the priests of the high places which he had made. So he offered upon the altar which he had made in Beth-el the fifteenth day of the eighth month, even in the month which he had devised of his own heart; and ordained a feast unto the children of Israel: and he offered upon the altar, and burnt incense.*

When I consider this, I think about what is going on in so many churches today where people think, "We need something new. We need to come up with something that is more exciting. This old stuff about God and the Bible is outdated; we need to bring this church up to modern-day life." So men devise things out of their own hearts and build worship around those things. God said, "When Jeroboam commanded you to worship these calves and not to go to Jerusalem, you obeyed him! You should never have done that."

There are many people whose senses have been dulled. Though they at first were wide awake in some of these churches, they then began to say, "You know, I don't really like all this music without Christ, but I guess it is what we have to get used to." A lady sitting next to me on a flight said, "It took me at least three months to adjust to my new church. The drama and the music so often take the place of teaching and preaching the Bible."

There comes a time when the threshold has been crossed, when all the boundaries have been ignored, and the Lord speaks to us through affliction. The only way we really give our burdens to the Lord is when they become so heavy that we can no longer carry them. We all wish that it were not that way, but all of us behave basically the same way.

# THE AFFLICTION OF THE MOTH

The moth became God's messenger. Hosea 5:12 says, *"Therefore will I be unto Ephraim as a moth, and to the house of Judah as rottenness."* Rottenness is something that works more slowly. He is including Judah in this judgment. Judah will go later into Babylonian captivity, but Israel will go into Assyrian captivity much sooner. He says, "The affliction I am going to send to you is as a moth."

I think all of us know about the creature we refer to as a moth. Occasionally, we see their work in our closets. Not too long ago, I went to retrieve a pair of black wool pants. I got the pants, put them on, and started to go out the door, when my wife said, "Hold it! The preacher does not need to go out with holes in his britches!" I said, "What are you talking about?" She said, "I want you to look! I see your legs through those pants!" A moth had eaten holes in them. That little creature had been in there quietly working away, destroying a perfectly good pair of pants!

The Lord said, "I want you to understand, this is a simple little creature. You never know that he is at work, but he is eating away. When you finally take notice that something has been destroyed, I want you to see my hand in it." Notice how He states this, *"Therefore will I be unto Ephraim as a moth."* He says, "I am going to come after you like a moth: silently, subtly eating away."

Beloved, we can see where the moths have eaten in our nation. A much more casual type of Christianity has eased its way into our lives.

We have grown weak and become accustomed to the darkness. We have found some rational way to explain why we do not resist evil like we once did. We are more sympathetic with those who are against the cause of Christ. The moths keep eating, and we grow weaker and weaker.

Dr. John Phillips has said that the first generation of Christians has real *convictions*. The second generation of Christians, the children of the first generation, has what they call *beliefs*. They have grown up in a Christian home and have heard it all their lives. In the third generation, we find they are most often only left with *opinions*.

*The only way we really give our burdens to the Lord is when they become so heavy that we can no longer carry them.*

How do we keep from being motheaten? Every generation must know God for themselves. They must exercise their own faith. If I kept my sons from all risk and all danger, and would not allow them to exercise in any way their manhood, I would not make them stronger. I would make than weaker.

The same principle applies to faith. Your children and grandchildren must exercise their own faith in God. They have to discover who God is for themselves. God has no grandchildren. We do, but God does not. God only has children.

I want a strong, robust faith. Do you? Put the Christian faith in the very center of the conflict. You do not have to fear the truth. We have the truth!

I meet some so-called Christian educators who have wrong ideas about Christian education. They are not making children stronger; they are weakening them. They build fences around them and box them in so that they cannot come into contact with anything that requires faith. The young people have been so confined they cannot confront anything. I know that these educators are trying to protect

children, but let us not be afraid of what God is able to do in someone's life! Young people must learn to exercise faith and trust the Lord.

Some have taken this to the extreme in their own life. It is as if they have built a bubble around themselves. They live in a bubble. Friends, that is not realistic, and it does not build strong faith. I am not talking about throwing people to the wolves; I am talking about trusting God, teaching the Bible, and helping people to understand the truth. We must pray with people and teach them to pray. We must trust God, and teach people to believe Him for themselves. So often, we live the faith life for our children and grandchildren and do not allow them to develop their own faith. This moth-eating should wake us up.

# THE AFFLICTION OF THE LION

Lions bring advanced affliction when compared to the moth.

Hosea 5:13-14 says,

> *When Ephraim saw his sickness, and Judah saw his wound, then went Ephraim to the Assyrian, and sent to king Jareb: yet could he not heal you, nor cure you of your wound. For I will be unto Ephraim as a lion, and as a young lion to the house of Judah: I, even I, will tear and go away; I will take away, and none shall rescue him.* (Hosea 5:13-14)

We have opportunity to seek God because of what the moths have eaten; we can come to God in our affliction. But if in our weakness we put confidence in men, then the lion will arrive.

Notice the emphasis God places on *"I."* He says, "I am going to attack you like a lion and tear you to pieces. I am going to leave a bloody mess! There is going to be turmoil and disaster that is much more pronounced than what a moth has eaten." A moth is one thing,

slowly eating away in a closet somewhere destroying something valuable; but a lion on the loose, ripping limbs and causing bloody wounds, is another thing entirely. God says, "If the moth does not work, then the lion is going to be loosed."

As a nation, we have seen the lion loosed in times of war, and churches filled with people seeking the Lord. Some of you have seen the lion loosed in your life. God says, "I am going to loose the lion to afflict you, not because I hate you, but because I love you." Even the lion's affliction did not bring them to the Lord in Hosea's day.

# THE AFFLICTION BROUGHT ON BY THE LORD LEAVING

What happens when God is gone? Hosea 5:15 says, *"I will go and return to my place, till they acknowledge their offence, and seek my face: in their affliction they will seek me early."* We come now to the affliction brought on by God leaving. He said, "I am going to remove my presence."

We know that God is omnipresent. He cannot remove Himself. He is using this language here to emphasize something. Where is God now?

At times, I have learned how to have a church meeting without the Lord. I have learned how to preach without God. It was miserable, but I learned to do it. I should never have learned to do it. How many of you sing Christian songs and learn to sing without God's enabling? How many of you teach the Bible and learn to do it without God's enabling? We learn to go through the motions. After a while, we become so weary.

When God withdraws His presence, certain things go with Him. The joy goes. In His presence is fullness of joy. When God leaves, the blessings are gone. When God leaves, holiness is gone. When people lack reverence for God and mock at sin, the real problem is that God is gone.

Wisdom leaves when God leaves. People start making terrible decisions. Life is about making right decisions. Everything becomes such a laborious, grueling task without God. The Christian life is supposed to be a faith life.

The Lord says, "If you want to live without Me, you will find out what it is really like to live without My blessing, without My holiness, and without My joy and peace. You will learn what it is like to live without My power. You will learn what it is like to live without My wisdom. I am leaving!"

We are living in the great *"till."* There is hope. Hosea 5:15 says, *"I will go and return to my place, till they acknowledge their offence, and seek my face: in their affliction they will seek me early."* Notice that little word *"till."* Thank God for this *"till."*

Perhaps you are thinking, "Lord, when are you coming back? When are you going to return and bless us and be in our family again like you once were? Lord, when will your hand of blessing be upon our ministry like it once was?" God said, "I am removing my presence...*till they acknowledge their offence."* This is repentance. We must repent and say, "I have sinned. I have learned how to live in the energy of the flesh. I have sinned; Lord, help me!" Then He says, *"...and seek my face."* That is faith! Then He says again, *"...in their affliction they will seek me early."*

Let us be honest with God. Get off that low standard. Recognize the moth-eaten life that is weakening us before the ravaging of the lion comes and the withdrawal of God takes place. Come in the light affliction! Come back to the Lord!

# CHAPTER SIX

# MURDER BY CONSENT

urder can be committed many ways, and those who consent to the crime are most evil. The Giver of Life is most offended by those who consent to commit murder. The well-known Puritan writer, Thomas Watson, wrote that murder could be committed with the hand; with the mind (hating a brother); with the tongue (speaking a murderous word); with the pen (David's note concerning Uriah); by plotting another's death (Jezebel plotting Naboth's death); by placing poison into cups; by witchcraft and sorcery; by intending to kill if possible; by consenting to another's death; by not stopping the death of another when it is in one's power to stop it; by unmercifulness; and by not executing the law upon capital offenders.

In the sixth chapter of the book of Hosea, God explains to us the absolute depravity of the people, the thoroughness of their sin, and the wickedness that God saw. Hosea 6:1-11 says,

> *Come, and let us return unto the LORD: for he hath torn, and he will heal us; he hath smitten, and he will bind us up. After two days will he revive us: in the*

*third day he will raise us up, and we shall live in his sight. Then shall we know, if we follow on to know the LORD: his going forth is prepared as the morning; and he shall come unto us as the rain, as the latter and former rain unto the earth.*

*O Ephraim, what shall I do unto thee? O Judah, what shall I do unto thee? for your goodness is as a morning cloud, and as the early dew it goeth away. Therefore have I hewed them by the prophets; I have slain them by the words of my mouth: and thy judgments are as the light that goeth forth. For I desired mercy, and not sacrifice; and the knowledge of God more than burnt-offerings. But they like men have transgressed the covenant: there have they dealt treacherously against me.*

*Gilead is a city of them that work iniquity, and is polluted with blood. And as troops of robbers wait for a man, so the company of priests murder in the way by consent: for they commit lewdness. I have seen an horrible thing in the house of Israel: there is the whoredom of Ephraim, Israel is defiled. Also, O Judah, he hath set an harvest for thee, when I returned the captivity of my people.*

Notice an expression in the ninth verse, *"murder...by consent."* Israel was to be the nation nearest to God, and the people in Israel nearest to God were to be the priests. God says, "When I look at this nation, my people Israel, their priests are murderers, and they murder by consent."

That word *"consent"* is an interesting word. Of course we know that it means that they all agreed to do this. It also reveals that their actions were predetermined and premeditated. Instead of doing

what priests should be doing in honoring God, these priests were murdering by consent.

I do not know all the reasons that God chose this visual word picture for us to depict the depravity of these people; but can you imagine the Lord saying concerning Christian leaders that you know, that they had all become a band of murderers by consent? This is something like the message we are dealing with in the prophecy of Hosea.

In the fifth chapter, the Lord leads up to this judgment. He tells the people that He is going to judge them by the moth (verse twelve), by the lion (verse fourteen), and by His absence (verse fifteen). The Lord says, "I have dealt with you as a moth, silently working and weakening. You should be wide-awake to what is going on, but you are not." So the Lord intensifies His judgment. He says, "I send a lion. When the lion comes, I am going to rip you apart. You are going to see the bloodshed and the misery brought on by the lion." Still, there was no moving toward the Lord. God says, "Then I cannot do anything more severe than this. I will be gone. I have blessed my people, given them wisdom, and provided them protection; but I am going to withdraw my hand of blessing and protection. I am going away. I will go and return to my place."

*We ought to stop and praise God that there is a way back to Him. The reason there is a way back is because Jesus Christ made the way.*

Then He gives us this beautiful word *"till."* That is a word of hope. He said, "I am leaving *'till'* you acknowledge your offense and seek my face." So God left the door open for His people to return to Him. As we enter into the sixth chapter, the Lord is waiting in that *"till."*

# THE PROPHET'S INVITATION

If you are willing to acknowledge your offense and come to the Lord, God is waiting. He has left the door open. He says, *"In their affliction they will seek me."*

The prophet says, as he speaks for the Lord in Hosea 6:1-2, *"Come, and let us return unto the LORD: for he hath torn, and he will heal us; he hath smitten, and he will bind us up. After two days will he revive us: in the third day he will raise us up, and we shall live in his sight."* There is absolutely nothing in Scripture that relates to this as well as the death, burial and resurrection of Jesus Christ. Of course, this passage was written hundreds of years before the time of Christ's coming; but in the mind of our God, the Lord Jesus Christ is the Lamb of God slain from the foundation of the world. This is a hopeful message the prophet is extending. This is God's invitation by way of His man. He is declaring to them, *"After two days will he revive us: in the third day he will raise us up, and we shall live in his sight."* He is talking here not only about what we have in Christ, but also what He is going to do for His people Israel.

The Bible says in verse three, *"Then shall we know, if we follow on to know the LORD: his going forth is prepared as the morning; and he shall come unto us as the rain, as the latter and former rain unto the earth."* God's people knew the necessity of rain because in a unique way, God placed His people in a land bridge between three continents, where there was very little fresh water available. Rain was absolutely necessary for life.

When you read the Bible, you find that in times of judgment God would cause severe droughts in the land. He would withhold the rain. Israel had two different seasons of rain. People knew that the rain was God's blessing and provision. The Lord had, no doubt, withheld the rain.

God said that He would send the rain to bless Israel. In other words, God is passionately bending over the balcony of glory, pleading with His people, "Come to Me and acknowledge your sin! Confess it! The invitation is extended."

This beautiful word is given with tenderness, *"Come, and let us return unto the LORD."* We ought to stop and praise God that there is a way back to Him. The reason there is a way back is because Jesus Christ made the way.

In Luke 13:6 we read, *"He spake also this parable; A certain man had a fig tree planted in his vineyard; and he came and sought fruit thereon, and found none."* This man had a fig tree in his vineyard. The fig tree pictures the nation of Israel. The fig tree should be bearing fruit, just as Israel should be bearing fruit. He had every reason to expect to find fruit, but the Bible says that He found none.

The Lord continues in verse seven, *"Then said he unto the dresser of his vineyard, Behold, these three years I come seeking fruit on this fig tree, and find none: cut it down; why cumbereth it the ground?"*

As the Lord Jesus tells this story, He is saying to His people, "You are like that fig tree." God has every reason to expect that you would bear fruit, that you would know the Lord, and that other people would come to the Lord because of you.

It is easy to see how this applies to God's people today. If we truly know the Lord, then other people should come to know the Lord by the fruit that we bear. When the Lord examined this fig tree, He found that there was no fruit. He said, "This tree is cumbering the ground and taking space where something could grow and be fruitful." When the Lord sees that there is no fruit, He says, *"Cut it down."*

I think that when Christ gave this story, He had a tone of such severity when He said, *"Cut it down."* But then immediately, there was a tone of such passion and pathos that followed in verses eight and nine. *"And he answering said unto him, Lord, let it alone this year also, till I shall dig about it, and dung it: and if it bear fruit, well: and if not, then after that thou shalt cut it down."*

He says, "Could you give us just a year? Let us dig about it and disturb the soil. Let us dung it and add the nutrients it needs. Let us have another opportunity. Extend mercy just one more year. Then, we will examine it when the fruit season arrives; if there is no fruit, then we will cut it down."

> *I wonder how many of God's people sit in church and take up a space on a pew and have no intention of ever doing anything to honor God?*

Even with the shadow of captivity hanging over the people of Israel in the book of Hosea, and even though God had already revealed the sinful condition of His people, He still instructs Hosea to say to them once again, "Come home!" God is waiting; acknowledge your sin and come back to Him.

I wonder how many of God's people sit in church and take up a space on a pew and have no intention of ever doing anything to honor God? How long will He allow us to cumber the ground? Do you ever believe that God is digging and dunging in your life? Is He disturbing the soil and adding spiritual nutrition so that you might once again have the opportunity to be fruitful for His glory?

Throughout our nation's history of sending missionaries and getting out the gospel, we have had a great purpose as a country. If we lose that and lay aside what God has given us to do, then we have no purpose as a people. How long will God let us continue?

How many will try to explain why there is no blessing and why good things that once happened are no longer happening? We are just like the tree that should be bearing fruit, but there is no fruit. How long will God allow the door to stay open? It is a misrepresentation of the truth to say, "We are God's people," and yet not yield to Him.

# THE LORD'S DESIRE

Now God speaks and He is disturbed. This is a very perplexing thing that is somewhat difficult to understand. Hosea 6:4 says, *"O Ephraim, what shall I do unto thee? O Judah, what shall I do unto thee? for your goodness is as a morning cloud, and as the early dew it goeth away."*

Remember, Ephraim is the prominent tribe in the northern kingdom. God uses this name to speak of all Israel. Judah is the southern kingdom. We know that the prophet Hosea is preaching to the northern kingdom of Israel. They will go into Assyrian captivity. Later, the southern kingdom of Judah will go into Babylonian captivity.

God declares His desire to do something! It is like a father saying to his erring children, "I want to help you! I want to bless you! I want to provide for you, but look how you are living! What am I going to do with you? *'What shall I do unto thee?'"*

He goes on to explain, *"...for your goodness is as a morning cloud, and as the early dew it goeth away."* In other words, you give some appearance of intending to do right. A morning cloud brings promise, but never fulfills its promise. The early dew would look like it is something worthwhile, but soon the heat of the sun dries it up. He says, "There are moments when it seems you are going to do right, but you never follow through with it. There are moments when it looks like you are going to turn and come to Me, but you never follow through."

As the Spirit of God works in our lives, trying time after time to gain our attention and draw us to Himself, how many times does He say, "For a moment, it looked like he was coming home. There was a moment when it looked like she was going to become earnest about her Christian life. There was a moment when it looked like that church was going to seek My face and do the right thing. There are moments like the morning cloud or early dew." Again and again it happens, but then it is gone. As desperately as God desires to bless us, He cannot bless us in that condition.

Isaiah 5:1-2 says,

> *Now will I sing to my wellbeloved a song of my beloved touching his vineyard. My wellbeloved hath a vineyard in a very fruitful hill: and he fenced it, and gathered out the stones thereof, and planted it with the choicest vine, and built a tower in the midst of it, and also made a winepress therein: and he looked that it should bring forth grapes, and it brought forth wild grapes.*

God said, "I gave so much attention to My vineyard. I did everything to make it fruitful." I want to stop for a moment and ask you, What more could God have done for us? What more could God have done for Israel? What more could God have done for Judah? Is there anyone who could stand to his or her feet and say in all earnestness, "God has mistreated me"? Can you breathe God's air and drink the water that God provides and walk around in the body that God designed to function and dare say that God could have done more?

Isaiah 3:3-7 says,

> *And now, O inhabitants of Jerusalem, and men of Judah, judge, I pray you, betwixt me and my vineyard. What could have been done more to my vineyard, that I have not done in it? wherefore, when I looked that it should bring forth grapes, brought it forth wild grapes? And now go to; I will tell you what I will do to my vineyard: I will take away the hedge thereof, and it shall be eaten up; and break down the wall thereof, and it shall be trodden down: and I will lay it waste: it shall not be pruned, nor digged; but*

*there shall come up briers and thorns: I will also command the clouds that they rain no rain upon it. For the vineyard of the LORD of hosts is the house of Israel, and the men of Judah his pleasant plant: and he looked for judgment, but behold oppression; for righteousness, but behold a cry.*

This is the dilemma that God is in. The Lord desires to bless and use us and shower upon us all the good things that He desires for us, but not in our sin.

The Bible says in Hosea 6:5-6, *"Therefore have I hewed them by the prophets; I have slain them by the words of my mouth: and thy judgments are as the light that goeth forth. For I desired mercy, and not sacrifice; and the knowledge of God more than burnt-offerings."* This is God's desire. He wants mercy. But they had become murderers *"by consent."* Their hearts were hardened.

Remember in chapter four, the Lord said that His problem was that when He looked in the land there was no truth, no mercy, and no knowledge of God. God says, "I want truth, I want mercy, and I want the knowledge of God, not this meaningless routine that you call worship. It is not worship at all."

I heard Dr. Vance Havner say years ago that we have a dynamite faith, and yet we live such little firecracker lives. God desires and longs to bless us; His heart moves toward us. What could God have done more?

# THE PEOPLE'S SIN

Hosea 6:7 says, *"But they like men have transgressed the covenant: there have they dealt treacherously against me."* All our sin is against God. We may sin against humanity, but is it in reality, against God. You may not treat your fellow man the way you ought

91

to, but in reality, your sin is against God. You may not treat your wife or husband the way you ought to, but in reality, you are sinning against God. You may dishonor your parents, but in reality, you dishonored God. God says, "You have transgressed against Me!" When we recognize that our sin is against God, then we must seek God for the forgiveness and help we need.

Hosea 6:8 says, *"Gilead is a city of them that work iniquity, and is polluted with blood."* All through the Bible when Gilead is mentioned, God says it is a city where there is a balm, a healing ointment. Here, the Lord tells us that Gilead is a city of sinful workers.

Jeremiah 8:20-22 says, *"The harvest is past, the summer is ended, and we are not saved. For the hurt of the daughter of my people am I hurt; I am black; astonishment hath taken hold on me. Is there no balm in Gilead; is there no physician there? why then is not the health of the daughter of my people recovered?"* A certain ointment was prepared in this place of Gilead, and it was used as a healing ointment. God says, "Is there no balm? Is there no healing ointment left?" The answer is yes. Then why is it not applied?

In the thirty-seventh chapter of Genesis, when Joseph's brethren decided they were going to sell Joseph to the merchantmen who were passing through, do you remember where those merchantmen were coming from? These Ishmaelites were coming from Gilead, and they were carrying the balm of Gilead.

It is no accident that God says to us that we are to look in Gilead for a balm for healing. But when you look in this land for healing, you do not find any healing. He says, "What you find in Gilead is a city of them that work iniquity. It has polluted their blood."

I wonder how many times God has looked in a place to find healing, but He found that it was polluted with blood instead. How many times has God looked in my life and found something dishonoring when He should have found something Christ-honoring? It is so easy to confess the sins of other people and other nations, but we must confess our own sins to God. *"If we confess our sins, he is faithful and just to forgive us our sins, and to cleanse us from all unrighteousness"* (I John 1:9). This is a message about Israel, but it is a message to all of us.

Hosea 6:9 says, *"And as troops of robbers wait for a man, so the company of priests murder in the way by consent: for they commit lewdness."* This was supposed to be a place of help and healing. It was supposed to be a place of the preaching and teaching of God's Word. Instead, it had become a gathering place of robbers and priests who murdered by consent.

*The Lord desires to bless and use us and shower upon us all the good things that He desires for us, but not in our sin.*

I want you to know something that is a little hard to take and is hard for me to express. There are many churches that are supposed to be places of help and healing, but they are murdering. They are giving people everything but God and God's Word.

A preacher friend in Texas took me on a tour of Fort Hood. He pointed out the vast area where they do military maneuvers. He explained that there are cattle ranches out there, and if by chance the military happens to kill a cow, the military must replace the cow for five generations. I said, "You mean, if you kill one cow, you have to replace the cow with five cows?" He said, "No, that is not what I said." He said, "They literally compute how many cows that cow could have had, and then how many cows those cows could have had, and how many cows those cows could have had up to five generations. If one cow is killed, the rancher gets a herd back!"

As I thought about that story, a haunting thought came to me. If I misrepresent God to one child, that child's life could be affected adversely. But it would affect more than his life alone. It would affect his home, his children, his children's children, his children's children's children, and so on.

There are murderers in churches who have cut off the truth and gone into the entertainment business and turned from God to *"another gospel"* (II Corinthians 11:4). Think of the generations of blood that will be on their hands when they meet God! So much damage is done so quickly.

> *There are murderers in churches who have cut off the truth and gone into the entertainment business and turned from God to* "another gospel." *Think of the generations of blood that will be on their hands when they meet God!*

We ought to fear God in such a way that we fear what sin does. The Bible says in Hosea 6:9-10, *"And as troops of robbers wait for a man, so the company of priests murder in the way by consent: for they commit lewdness. I have seen an horrible thing in the house of Israel: there is the whoredom of Ephraim, Israel is defiled."*

God says, "I see a horrible thing in the house of Israel. I should see a blessed thing; I should see a wonderful thing. I should look and see God-glorifying things." But God says, "I looked and have seen a horrible thing. There is whoredom. Israel is defiled."

The judgment is going to fall, and the Lord gives great detail leading up to it. No one will shake his finger in the face of God and say, "We did not deserve this!" I wonder about our beloved country, my own life, and the church which I have the privilege to pastor. What does God see when He looks at us?

Hosea 6:11 says, *"Also, O Judah, he hath set an harvest for thee, when I returned the captivity of my people."* Suddenly, there is a ray of light and hope. God talks about the return of His people. He is saying, "There is still hope."

The southern kingdom of Judah will go into captivity, and God will put in the heart of a captor to let them go. This is unheard of, but God will do that. Psalm 126:1 says, *"When the LORD turned again the captivity of Zion, we were like them that dream."* God said, "I am going to do it. That is how it can be!"

Some of you may think, "I have wasted every opportunity that God has given me. I have made a mess of my life, my marriage, and my children's lives." Some of you are tormented thinking about all of the wreckage. God says, "There is a door of hope open for you."

As long as there is life, there is hope. God is going to give you an opportunity to invest your life wisely. God can restore the years that the locust has eaten (Joel 2:25); that is what He told the prophet Joel. Because you are alive, God has given you a time of extended mercy and opportunity.

Some of you can be so thankful, with the mess that you have made, that God took the broken clay and made it over again. He has become so sweet and precious to you. In the midst of sin, darkness, and depravity, God extends mercy.

# Chapter Seven

# Unaware

ost people who have been diagnosed with terminal illnesses were totally unaware of their serious conditions until the doctor informed them. The Great Physician reveals the dying condition of a nation, and to make matters even worse, they were completely unaware. As we travel through the book of Hosea, we come to a terribly tragic chapter. We are left with nothing to do but to deal with this terminal sin sickness head-on and pray that God will use it to speak to our hearts. The Bible says in Hosea 7:1-16,

> *When I would have healed Israel, then the iniquity of Ephraim was discovered, and the wickedness of Samaria: for they commit falsehood; and the thief cometh in, and the troop of robbers spoileth without. And they consider not in their hearts that I remember all their wickedness: now their own doings have beset them about; they are before my face. They make the king glad with their wickedness, and the princes with their lies. They are all adulterers, as an oven heated*

by the baker, who ceaseth from raising after he hath kneaded the dough, until it be leavened. In the day of our king the princes have made him sick with bottles of wine; he stretched out his hand with scorners. For they have made ready their heart like an oven, whiles they lie in wait: their baker sleepeth all the night; in the morning it burneth as a flaming fire. They are all hot as an oven, and have devoured their judges; all their kings are fallen: there is none among them that calleth unto me.

Ephraim, he hath mixed himself among the people; Ephraim is a cake not turned. Strangers have devoured his strength, and he knoweth it not: yea, gray hairs are here and there upon him, yet he knoweth not. And the pride of Israel testifieth to his face: and they do not return to the LORD their God, nor seek him for all this. Ephraim also is like a silly dove without heart: they call to Egypt, they go to Assyria. When they shall go, I will spread my net upon them; I will bring them down as the fowls of the heaven; I will chastise them, as their congregation hath heard.

Woe unto them! for they have fled from me: destruction unto them! because they have transgressed against me: though I have redeemed them, yet they have spoken lies against me. And they have not cried unto me with their heart, when they howled upon their beds: they assemble themselves for corn and wine, and they rebel against me. Though I have bound and strengthened their arms, yet do they imagine mischief against me. They return, but not to the most High: they are like a deceitful bow: their princes shall fall

*by the sword for the rage of their tongue: this shall be their derision in the land of Egypt.*

We read in the ninth verse, *"...he knoweth it not."* This expression occurs twice in this verse. The people were unaware of their decadence. They were unaware of their loss of strength and of their true standing with God. They knew they had sinned, but they were unaware of how totally desperate their situation was.

If I had an illness that would take my life, but it was not identified by pain and was difficult to diagnose, then I would know it was extremely dangerous.

> *As the Lord looked at His people, He saw that they were unaware of their spiritual loss. They were unaware of how far they had drifted and how distant they were from God.*

As the Lord looked at His people, He saw that they were unaware of their spiritual loss. They were unaware of how far they had drifted and how distant they were from God.

They had rationalized in their minds that if they were going through the motions and portraying a religious appearance, then all was well. But all was not well! Their strength was gone. *"Gray hairs"* were here and there, and they did not know it. There is not one of us who has gray hair that does not remember when we started getting the first few of those. God uses this to illustrate something, calling attention to something deeply and spiritually wrong.

The Bible says in verse nine, *"Strangers have devoured his strength, and he knoweth it not: yea, gray hairs are here and there upon him, yet he knoweth not."* In the natural realm there is not one of us who would not know that we had gray hair, but God says, "I am speaking here of spiritual things. Death is coming on you. Decay is already setting in. You are nearing the end, and you are unaware!"

People often think that they would like for God to remove the curtain and enable them to see the future, but I do not think any of us have enough grace to deal with that. Rudyard Kipling, the famous author, took a trip to America with his little daughter Josephine. They laughed and had the greatest time on board the boat all during their travel, but shortly after that trip ended, his little darling daughter died. If he had known during that trip how short her time was, I doubt seriously if he could have had any enjoyment at all while traveling on that voyage.

*There are many who still attend church, say their prayers before their meals, and habitually read passages from the Bible. They still talk like Christians, and they give answers to people like Christian people give answers; but God's power and blessing is gone.*

I do not know how near our nation is to destruction, but I do believe that as a nation, we are unaware. I do not know how close some of God's people are to severe chastening as a result of their rebellion against God, but I know that many of them are very unaware of how near they are.

God spoke through His prophet to the nation of Israel, "You are unaware." He told them, "When I would have healed Israel, then the iniquity of Ephraim was discovered." The Lord is not willing that any should perish, but that all should come to repentance.

Consider the example of Samson. Samson was a man separated to God. That is what his Nazarite vow was all about. He was a mighty man. I do not believe for a moment that he looked like a man of

extraordinary strength, because no one could discover the secret of his might. It was God in his life.

Certainly, Samson was a man blessed of God. The Bible says in Judges 14:6, *"And the Spirit of the LORD came mightily upon him."* That is when he killed a lion with his bare hands. Verse nineteen says, *"And the Spirit of the LORD came upon him."* This was the slaying of the men at Ashkelon. The Bible says in Judges 15:14, *"And the Spirit of the LORD came mightily upon him."* Here Samson slew a thousand men with the jawbone of an animal.

In Judges chapter sixteen, after Samson has revealed his heart to Delilah and broken his vow to God, notice what verse twenty says, *"And he awoke out of his sleep, and said, I will go out as at other times before, and shake myself. And he wist not that the LORD was departed from him."* He thought, "I will do what I have always done." But something had happened in his heart that caused him to lose God's blessing on his life. He was unaware that God's power was gone. I never read that without praying, "Lord, make me aware!"

There are many who still attend church, say their prayers before their meals, and habitually read passages from the Bible. They still talk like Christians, and they give answers to people like Christian people give answers; but God's power and blessing is gone. Are you aware or are you unaware?

Hosea 7:2 says, *"And they consider not in their hearts that I remember all their wickedness."* The Lord looks directly into the heart, and sees that they do not consider that He remembers their wickedness.

The Bible teaches a great truth that God forgets our confessed sins, and He remembers them no more. They are cast behind God's back (Isaiah 38:17). It is wonderful and glorious when sin is gone and forgotten. But God says that when sin is unconfessed and never dealt with, He looks into our heart and sees our sin.

Hosea 7:2-3 says, *"And they consider not in their hearts that I remember all their wickedness: now their own doings have beset them about; they are before my face. They make the king glad with their wickedness, and the princes with their lies."* He says, "The king is involved in the wickedness, and all of the people are involved in wickedness. They are so unaware of the dangerous predicament that their sin has brought them into."

We need to pray that God would keep us alert and sensitive to the moving of His Spirit. We have a gracious God who does not let us go on in our own way without dealing with us.

# THEY ARE AN OVEN

The Lord says in Hosea 7:4, *"They are all adulterers, as an oven heated by the baker, who ceaseth from raising after he hath kneaded the dough, until it be leavened."* Notice the word *"adulterers"* here, because God is connecting this heated situation with sexual sin. When idolatry comes in, immorality is soon to follow. When people displace God in their lives and no longer see the Lord high, exalted, and lifted up, then immorality is soon to follow. Immorality is always preceded by idolatry.

Verse five continues, *"In the day of our king the princes have made him sick with bottles of wine; he stretched out his hand with scorners."* In other words, the king is inviting them in with an outstretched hand; he is inviting them in to join him in his sin.

Verse six says, *"For they have made ready their heart like an oven, whiles they lie in wait: their baker sleepeth all the night; in the morning it burneth as a flaming fire."* The oven is heated hot all the night; even early in the morning, it is burning as a flaming fire.

*"They are all hot as an oven, and have devoured their judges; all their kings are fallen: there is none among them that calleth unto*

*me.''* When the Lord looked upon His people who were to be a holy people and to reflect the righteousness of God, they were a flaming fire of adultery and immorality. They were as an oven. Think of their behavior!

Remember that our God is a holy God. He says to His people, *"Be ye holy; for I am holy"* (I Peter 1:16).

# THEY ARE LIKE A CAKE NOT TURNED

Hosea 7:8 says, *"Ephraim, he hath mixed himself among the people; Ephraim is a cake not turned."* Notice the word *"mixed."* He speaks of intermarriage of believers marrying unbelievers. It was no longer important to God's people for their children who believe to grow up and marry believers. The standard had been lost. If we do not guard this vigilantly and teach our children this, it is going to be lost for us as well.

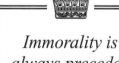

*Immorality is always preceded by idolatry.*

Joshua 23:10-13 says,

> *One man of you shall chase a thousand: for the* LORD *your God, he it is that fighteth for you, as he hath promised you. Take good heed therefore unto yourselves, that ye love the* LORD *your God. Else if ye do in any wise go back, and cleave unto the remnant of these nations, even these that remain among you, and shall make marriages with them, and go in unto them, and they to you: know for a certainty that the* LORD *your God will no more drive out any of these nations from before you; but they shall be snares*

*and traps unto you, and scourges in your sides, and thorns in your eyes, until ye perish from off this good land which the LORD your God hath given you.*

The Lord told them that if believers began to marry unbelievers, God would drive them out of the land. There may be some people who disagree with applying this word given to Israel to God's people in this present time, but let us stop for a moment and give adequate consideration to it.

Do you believe the Bible to be God's eternal Word? Do you believe that our God is the only true and living God? Do you believe that His Son, the Lord Jesus Christ, is the only Saviour, and that there is no salvation apart from the Lord Jesus Christ? Then you have come also to some distinctive beliefs in your heart concerning God and God's work.

In our homes, we should bring up our children to adhere to true biblical standards. God's plan for them is to marry those who have the same true biblical standards, and to pass those convictions from one generation to the next. (Read Deuteronomy 6:1-7.)

The Bible says in the book of Judges that *"There arose another generation after them, which knew not the LORD, nor yet the works which he had done"* (Judges 2:10). The reason there arose a generation which knew not the Lord is that they did not keep this sacred trust in their homes. This is not just advice; this is something that needs to be taken to heart and lived out in our homes.

If you are so unrealistic as to expect that you can train your children by simply bringing them to church, you are sadly mistaken. The church can never take the place of the training that you need to provide in your home. A church can reinforce and emphasize what you are trying to emphasize, but God's Word ought to be taught line upon line, precept upon precept, in your home. There ought to be times in your home when these things are discussed with your

children. God even tells us in His Word when to talk to children about these things (Deuteronomy 6:7).

Again, Hosea 7:8 says, *"Ephraim, he hath mixed himself among the people; Ephraim is a cake not turned." "A cake not turned"* is something that is half-baked. One side is burned and the other side is raw. It renders the cake useless. The cake could have been something nourishing, helpful, and healthful. It could have been something productive, but it was burned on one side and raw on the other, so it is now useless.

*The church can never take the place of the training that you need to provide in your home.*

Hosea 7:9 says, *"Strangers have devoured his strength, and he knoweth it not: yea, gray hairs are here and there upon him, yet he knoweth not."* In other words, He says, "You were once strong and mighty; you had God's strength. You were the bearers of the truth in a world that did not know the truth. God was your strength, but now your strength is gone." When did this happen? How did this take place?

When an unbeliever who does not know or love God is joined with someone who says that he or she is a believer who knows and loves God, they have joined themselves together with an impossible task. It is an impossible task to work together in such a union, in a wholehearted effort to bring another generation along to know the truth.

If you are a Christian and you marry an unbeliever, one of you is spiritually alive, and the other is spiritually dead. It is like marrying a corpse. There is an element of your life that can never be shared with an unbeliever, if you are truly a believer. In your life, there is an element that can never be communicated with an unbeliever, if you are a believer.

Believers ought to marry believers and teach their children the same truths and convictions that they have been taught. From one generation to the next, this truth is to be passed on. This is God's design. When people are heated like an oven, that does not happen.

The natural progression of an adulterous people is to break God's design for the home. Hosea 7:9-10 says, *"Strangers have devoured his strength, and he knoweth it not: yea, gray hairs are here and there upon him, yet he knoweth not. And the pride of Israel testifieth to his face: and they do not return to the LORD their God, nor seek him for all this."* God says, "Your family is breaking down; you are losing your children. Sexual immorality abounds. Everything is falling apart." God says, "For all of this, you are still not moved."

# THEY ARE LIKE A SILLY DOVE

Hosea 7:11 says, *"Ephraim also is like a silly dove without heart: they call to Egypt, they go to Assyria."* This word *"silly"* is an interesting word. It means "easily persuaded." Perhaps it meant at one time something giddy or joyful, but here it means "lacking judgment, easily persuaded, or led easily astray." He says, "My people are like a silly dove. They are easily led astray. They have no discernment."

God uses a word like this in the New Testament in II Timothy chapter three. He speaks about the corrupt characteristics of the last days, and He says in verse six, *"For of this sort are they which creep into houses, and lead captive silly women laden with sins, led away with divers lusts."* I do not know what you imagine a silly woman to be, but here it means exactly the same thing as in Hosea chapter seven. This is a woman who lacks judgment and is easily persuaded.

Many religious movements are built by leading *"silly"* women around. Before you start to blame the silly women who are being led astray, why do we not stop and admit what the real problem is: men have not risen up to be the spiritual leaders that they ought to be. If they were being the leaders they ought to be, we would not be seeing all of this. God says, "My people are like a silly dove." Look closely at where the silly dove goes.

Hosea 7:11 says, *"Ephraim also is like a silly dove without heart: they call to Egypt, they go to Assyria."* They should be going to the Lord. But they do not.

Verse twelve says, *"When they shall go, I will spread my net upon them; I will bring them down as the fowls of the heaven; I will chastise them, as their congregation hath heard."* We think that that is a terrible thing; no, it is a merciful thing that God did. Chastisement is an act of love. The Bible speaks of this as an act of love. God is dealing with His people through love.

Verse thirteen says, *"Woe unto them! for they have fled from me: destruction unto them! because they have transgressed against me: though I have redeemed them, yet they have spoken lies against me."* We should be fleeing to the Lord, but God

*Believers ought to marry believers and teach their children the same truths and convictions that they have been taught. From one generation to the next, this truth is to be passed on. This is God's design.*

says here, "My people have fled from Me!" We all act at times like silly doves. We behave with no judgment and no discernment. We should be seeking God, but we run from God, and we run for counsel to everyone else, our Egyptians and our Assyrians. We ask counsel of everyone but God. The Egyptians will lend us their tools and methods to make us more comfortable in Egypt. They will help us get settled down there. The Bible says, *"They have fled from me."*

Can you imagine these people, who once honored God, being so far gone that they are now speaking lies against God? Verse fourteen says, *"And they have not cried unto me with their heart, when they*

*howled upon their beds: they assemble themselves for corn and wine, and they rebel against me."* Notice the expression, *"with their heart."* God knows if we are speaking from our heart. Sometimes my vain repetitions make me sick; I can only imagine what they do to God.

One of my spiritual fathers, Dr. Frank Sells, used to say, "If we have the name of Jesus on our lips and do not have Him honored in our hearts, that is hypocrisy, and we have taken God's name in vain." Dear one, be careful about how you use the name of the Lord. Around your home, do not allow your children to use slang terms for the name of our God. Do not even allow slang words like "golly" or "gosh." Hold the name of God in such high reverence, honor, and respect that this is not a part of your vocabulary, and do not allow it in the lives of your children. Teach them the honor, respect, and reverence of God's name by your behavior.

*We all act at times like silly doves. We behave with no judgment and no discernment. We should be seeking God, but we run from God and we run for counsel to everyone else.*

The Bible says, *"And they have not cried unto me with their heart, when they howled upon their beds: they assemble themselves for corn and wine, and they rebel against me."* Like animals, they are howling, "Oh, things are awful! We are living in perilous times and facing terrible things! The entire world is in peril, and we are howling out about it." But God says, "They are not crying out to Me from their heart." Do you ever think about how much howling goes on in America and around the world concerning the awful conditions that we are facing today, but how little of that is actually crying out to God?

The way they dealt with all this trouble was to get drunk, forget their problems, have a good time, and dilute their minds. The world is constantly inviting us, especially our youth, to do the same.

The Word of God says in verse fifteen, *"Though I have bound and strengthened their arms, yet do they imagine mischief against me."* It is an awful thing to position one's self against the Lord.

# THEY ARE LIKE A DECEITFUL BOW

Hosea 7:16 says, *"They return, but not to the most High: they are like a deceitful bow: their princes shall fall by the sword for the rage of their tongue: this shall be their derision in the land of Egypt."* He said, "They return, but they do not return to God." Just when they would seek the Lord, the Devil offers something else instead of God.

There are people who grow sick of their life and sick of their sin, and God extends an invitation for them to come to Him. But just as they are moving toward Him, Satan offers a substitute. They say, "We cannot live like this forever; we have to change some things." They return, but not to the most high God.

God says, "They returned, but not to the Most High," and then He says, *"They are like a deceitful bow."* What does that mean? Imagine shooting a bow that never hits the mark. It never strikes where you aim. No matter how hard you try, it does not work right.

I wonder if you and I are willing to ask God, "Lord, if I continue the way I am going right now, will You show where I am headed?" Where are you headed? If you continue to do the same thing that you are doing right now with God, His Word, His church, and His Spirit, where will it take you? You may have convinced yourself that you are aiming at the Lord, but if you are not walking with Him daily, moment by moment, your aim is way off.

So they run to Egypt. In verse sixteen He says, *"Their princes shall fall by the sword for the rage of their tongue: this shall be their derision in the land of Egypt."* What is derision? It is to be laughed at and scorned. Some of you are thinking, "I have taken another

route. This Bible route, this holy life route, is not for me. It may have been for my mom and dad, but it is not for me." You want a different idea, a different way of doing things.

You have a bow that is deceitful. It is never going to hit the target. Not one of us is living perfectly, but we have found the perfect Book to follow. The Bible way and Bible truth is what we need to follow. May God help us to adhere to it.

God's people said, "We are not going to trust the Lord. We are trusting Egypt." God said, "Do you know what is going to become of you? The Egyptians you trust are going to laugh at you." I have seen good people get caught up in bad things, trying to gain the approval of those engaged in bad things. It does not take long until that person who was once respected is now derided.

*Where are you headed? If you continue to do the same thing that you are doing right now with God, His Word, His church, and His Spirit, where will it take you?*

What people respect about you is the decency in your talk, your dress, and in what you do with your body. If you start giving that up to be accepted, it will not be long before those same people who did have some respect for you will be holding you in derision and laughing at you. You will be just like them, if not worse. The Christian life is a holy life.

Many a girl and many a boy has gone into something sinful just to try to get someone's approval. They have lowered their standard and forgotten what the Bible says. They have chosen their own way. May God wake you up! Heed the warning He gives in an oven heated, a cake not turned, a silly dove, and a deceitful bow!

## CHAPTER EIGHT

# THEY HAVE SOWN THE WIND, AND THEY SHALL REAP THE WHIRLWIND

 od's Word teaches the law of sowing and reaping. The Bible declares in Galatians 6:8, *"For he that soweth to his flesh shall of the flesh reap corruption; but he that soweth to the Spirit shall of the Spirit reap life everlasting."* A college professor once said to me "Life is like a cafeteria line. As you walk through the line, you can take what you want; but always remember, at the end of the line you must pay for the choices you have made.

As we arrive at the eighth chapter of Hosea, the alarm is sounding loudly. It tells of the soon coming judgment of God.

The Bible says in Hosea 8:1-14,

> *Set the trumpet to thy mouth. He shall come as an eagle against the house of the LORD, because they have transgressed my covenant, and trespassed against my law. Israel shall cry unto me, My God, we know thee. Israel hath cast off the thing that is good: the enemy shall pursue him. They have set up kings,*

*but not by me: they have made princes, and I knew it not: of their silver and their gold have they made them idols, that they may be cut off.*

*Thy calf, O Samaria, hath cast thee off; mine anger is kindled against them: how long will it be ere they attain to innocency? For from Israel was it also: the workman made it; therefore it is not God: but the calf of Samaria shall be broken in pieces. For they have sown the wind, and they shall reap the whirlwind: it hath no stalk: the bud shall yield no meal: if so be it yield, the strangers shall swallow it up.*

*Israel is swallowed up: now shall they be among the Gentiles as a vessel wherein is no pleasure. For they are gone up to Assyria, a wild ass alone by himself: Ephraim hath hired lovers. Yea, though they have hired among the nations, now will I gather them, and they shall sorrow a little for the burden of the king of princes. Because Ephraim hath made many altars to sin, altars shall be unto him to sin. I have written to him the great things of my law, but they were counted as a strange thing. They sacrifice flesh for the sacrifices of mine offerings, and eat it; but the LORD accepteth them not; now will he remember their iniquity, and visit their sins: they shall return to Egypt. For Israel hath forgotten his Maker, and buildeth temples; and Judah hath multiplied fenced cities: but I will send a fire upon his cities, and it shall devour the palaces thereof.*

God says in verse seven, *"For they have sown the wind, and they shall reap the whirlwind."* Again, the Bibles says in Galatians 6:7, *"Be not deceived; God is not mocked: for whatsoever a man soweth,*

114

*that shall he also reap."* God said to His ancient people, Israel, "You have sown to the wind, and when you sow the wind, you are going to reap the whirlwind."

Beloved, we always reap more than we sow. We also reap the same thing we sow. We all sow and we all reap. The solemn conclusion is given at the end of this chapter, *"Israel hath forgotten his Maker."*

The only true and living God is "the forgotten God." How do people forget God? We cannot totally remove God from our thinking, no matter how hard we try. Our conscience bears witness to Him, and creation bears witness to Him, but the Bible says they have forgotten their Maker.

*The Bible is for all people for all time. Laws and standards of morality change; but God's Word never changes.*

As we begin this chapter, God says, *"Set the trumpet to thy mouth."* In other words, sound the trumpet and startle a sleeping people. They must wake up, for the judgment of God is upon them. Judgment must always begin at the house of God. It is so easy to go to sleep spiritually. May God keep us wide awake.

The Lord said, "I want my people awakened, so sound the trumpet." If they were sleeping in the night and an enemy approached, a certain sounding of the trumpet would mean, "Arise, and prepare for battle!" God is saying to His prophet, "You are that trumpet," and to His preachers, "You are that trumpet. Lift up your voice and herald forth the Word of God. Tell My people what I have to say!" We are to speak like a trumpet, clear, startling, and arousing. People must be alert and wide awake. *"Cry aloud, spare not, lift up thy voice like a trumpet, and shew my people their transgression, and the house of Jacob their sins"* (Isaiah 58:1).

Hosea 8:1 says, *"Set the trumpet to thy mouth. He shall come as an eagle against the house of the LORD, because they have transgressed my covenant, and trespassed against my law."* The enemy is coming as an eagle, swift, and powerful. He is speaking of the Assyrians coming and carrying them away captive. They thought this to be unimaginable. But God says, "The eagle is coming."

He also speaks to Judah in this chapter. They shall fall much later to the Babylonians led by Nebuchadnezzar. Their judgment is spoken of also, coming upon them swiftly and powerfully like an eagle. Then God says, *"because."* When God says *"because,"* take special notice. He begins to list things five things that bring about His judgment. Let us cover these things, and then come to the last verse where God summarizes it all. The heart of the matter is dealt with in the conclusion. Watch and pray. Carefully examine the *"because"* of God's judgment. These principles are timeless.

# THEY HAVE BROKEN MY LAW

Hosea 8:1 says, *"Set the trumpet to thy mouth. He shall come as an eagle against the house of the LORD, because they have transgressed my covenant, and trespassed against my law."* The Word of God is our fixed point of reference for all time and eternity. It never changes.

From generation to generation, people weaken the standards, but the Bible never changes. You cannot confine the Bible just to one generation. Your great-granddaddy may have believed the Bible, but you cannot say, "That was good for him, but it does not work in my day." The Bible is for all people for all time. Laws and standards of morality change; but God's Word never changes.

We live in a world of laws. We live in a civilized world, and we are to be law-abiding citizens in this civilized world. We live in a world that has some moral standards. They are always shifting and drifting to the left becoming looser and looser. Perhaps we can even say that we live in an amoral society where people say, "I make the rules for my life. I do as I please. What I say is right."

116

There is in every society moral middle ground. People say, "We will go this far and no further." But, evil men and seducers are always waxing worse and worse. What we held as a moral standard a generation ago has changed and drifted much further in the wrong direction.

We have laws and moral standards. Laws adjust to those moral standards. After a while, people can no longer control situations when things become so immoral, so they change the laws to accommodate the drifting moral standards. Things that were once criminal are no longer crimes. They were considered immoral and illegal, but laws have changed because of drifting moral standards.

The Bible never changes. It is not a cultural document. It is the Word of God. Believing people in every generation must say, "I am going to be guided by the Word of God. Whatever the world says is right, if it disagrees with the Bible, I am going to stay with the Bible." God always has a people. He had ancient Israel to abide by His law, and this set a standard for the rest of the world. The Word of God is our standard for living.

*When God's people ceased to be messengers of His truth, they had no reason to continue to exist. Our beloved nation ceases to have a reason for existence if we cease to be messengers of God to a lost world.*

Hosea 8:2 says, *"Israel shall cry unto me, My God, we know thee."* When the judgment comes, they are going to say, "But Lord, we are yours!" The Bible says in Matthew 7:22-23, *"Many will say to me in that day, Lord, Lord, have we not prophesied in thy name? and in thy name have cast out devils? and in thy name done many wonderful works? And then will I profess unto them, I never knew you: depart from me, ye that work iniquity."* They are going to say, "But Lord, we are your people!" and God is going to say, "You have broken my law. You have transgressed my covenant, and you have trespassed against my law."

Hosea 8:3 says, *"Israel hath cast off the thing that is good: the enemy shall pursue him."* People become despisers of those that are good. That is what the Bible says in II Timothy 3:3.

# THEY HAVE SET UP KINGS

The people chose their own standards for leaders while disregarding God's Word. Hosea 8:4 says, *"They have set up kings, but not by me: they have made princes, and I knew it not: of their silver and their gold have they made them idols, that they may be cut off."* They set up kings. They turned away from God's counsel concerning leaders.

> *God's Word is a most precious gift, but this precious gift was discarded.*

People today do not care who leads just as long as their personal interests are cared for. I am in a state of shock that some professing Christians are willing to support people and causes that totally disagree with the Word of God. What is more shocking is that they pass it off as nothing. God says, "I am going to judge my people for that."

# THEY HAVE BECOME A NATION OF IDOLATERS

The Bible says in Hosea 8:5, *"Thy calf, O Samaria, hath cast thee off; mine anger is kindled against them: how long will it be ere they attain to innocency?"* In other words, They made a calf to worship instead of God, and now this calf is doing them no good. Think of what we love that cannot love us in return? We are to love the Lord our God with all our heart.

Hosea 8:6 says, *"For from Israel was it also: the workman made it; therefore it is not God: but the calf of Samaria shall be broken in pieces."* If the workman made it, how can it be God? It is a creation of the workman. In fact, the workman is really the god of the idol.

Think of how many things made with men's hands have been turned into false gods. God told the people that they had become a nation of idolaters, and He would judge them. When God's people ceased to be messengers of His truth, they had no reason to continue to exist. Our beloved nation ceases to have a reason for existence if we cease to be messengers of God to a lost world. A nation of idolaters must be judged.

The Bible says in Hosea 8:7, *"For they have sown the wind, and they shall reap the whirlwind."* The small things that they neglected have become greater and greater. The tiny things that we neglect to do become giants of opposition all too soon. The tiny things we did that we should not have done become monsters with which we must do battle. *"They have sown the wind."* It seemed like a simple matter, but now they are going to reap more than they have ever sown. They are going to reap a *"whirlwind."*

The last part of Hosea 8:7 says, *"it hath no stalk: the bud shall yield no meal: if so be it yield, the strangers shall swallow it up."* God speaks here of a plant that has no stalk. In other words, it has every good appearance, but it has no nourishment in it. There is nothing in it to satisfy. They put all their efforts into something that brings no nourishment and no satisfaction. That is what idolatry is. Everything you have worked for and labored for is going to be taken by someone else.

Hosea 8:8 says, *"Israel is swallowed up: now shall they be among the Gentiles as a vessel wherein is no pleasure."* They were once such a glory to the Lord and to the nations. Now they are scattered among the Gentiles. Here we consider about the hated Jew. The apple of God's eye is now the hated Jew. We are to love Israel as God's people and pray for the peace of Jerusalem, but we all are well aware of the attitude the world has toward the Jew.

God asked His people, "Do you understand what you have done? You are scattered among the Gentiles, and you will be nothing but the hated Jews!"

# THEY FORSOOK THE LORD AND SOUGHT OTHERS FOR SAFETY

Our God is the Almighty God. There is need for no other. Hosea 8:9 says, *"For they are gone up to Assyria, a wild ass alone by himself: Ephraim hath hired lovers."* They are become like a wild animal with no one to care for it. They are hunted as prey by predators with no loving care. The wild animal is not an animal that is fed and cared for at all. This is a wild animal left to fend for itself, hunted and tracked by other beasts. The Lord is comparing His precious people to this animal. Think of the grief and passion in the heart of God as the prophet Hosea is preaching.

The Lord said, "Come unto me," but they ran to Assyria for help. They paid people to take care of them. They were not a people and God made them a people. But now they hire others to care for them.

The prophet goes on in Hosea 8:10, *"Yea, though they have hired among the nations, now will I gather them, and they shall sorrow a little for the burden of the king of princes."* We think that God is speaking here of the king of Assyria and the sorrow that they are about to face. No one could ever imagine the sorrow that awaits those who turn from the true God.

# THEY HAVE MADE MANY ALTARS

God's people are to worship God and God alone, but these people made many altars. Hosea 8:11 says, *"Because Ephraim hath made many altars to sin, altars shall be unto him to sin."* They took the truth of God's Word and made a false religion. They no longer proclaim the truth, but only their false religion. God must judge them for their lies.

The Bible says in Hosea 8:12, *"I have written to him the great things of my law, but they were counted as a strange thing."* Notice the expression *"great things of my law"* and *"strange thing."* God gave His Word to His people, Israel. God said, "I gave you the great things of the law, but you have turned the *'great things'* into a *'strange thing.'"*

> *We magnify our efforts and forget the Lord. We substitute everything imaginable for the place we should give God in our life.*

These people were the bearers of God's Holy Word. How did they treat it? The Bible says that they counted it as a *"strange thing."* A strange thing is something that does not belong to you. They did not want it. God's Word is a most precious gift, but this precious gift was discarded.

Are we willing to bear the reproach that comes with truly being a Bible-believing Christian in the midst of an unbelieving world? We should say, "My family adheres to God's Word. We identify ourselves with Jesus Christ and holy living." Before we are so hard on these Jews, we should take a long look at ourselves and let God speak to us.

God's chosen people decided they were not going to be identified with the Word of God. They counted it as a strange thing, as if it did not belong to them. God judged them for this.

*Do you realize what you are raising when you forget God in your home? As we forget God in our homes, we are raising a generation that will transgress God's Word and say that the Bible is not for us. We are raising a generation that will become a nation of idolaters.*

Hosea 8:13 says, *"They sacrifice flesh for the sacrifices of mine offerings, and eat it; but the LORD accepteth them not; now will he remember their iniquity, and visit their sins: they shall return to Egypt."* God speaks here of something literal, but also of captivity and bondage.

When He says that they make offerings, we realize that this is an attempt to say, "Wait a minute, Lord! Do not let this happen to us!" God says, "I will not accept it. It is too late." This is the preaching of the prophet Hosea. He told them that it was too late.

God summarizes this chapter in Hosea 8:14, *"For Israel hath forgotten his Maker, and buildeth temples; and Judah hath multiplied fenced cities: but I will send a fire upon his cities, and it shall devour the palaces thereof."* Notice, they forgot God and instead of depending on the Lord, they said, "We are going to fortify ourselves, secure ourselves, and be safe from our own doing." This is what all of us do when we forget the Lord.

What does this mean, *"Israel hath forgotten his Maker"*? This is God's conclusion concerning their sin. We have seen the five reasons that God said He was going to judge them, and in conclusion, He declares, "The reason for all this is that they forgot their Maker."

In the writing of Moses, the Lord instructed His people concerning their conduct in the land to which He would bring them. We read in Deuteronomy 4:9-10,

> *Only take heed to thyself, and keep thy soul diligently, lest thou forget the things which thine eyes have seen, and lest they depart from thy heart all the days of thy life: but teach them thy sons, and thy sons' sons; specially the day that thou stoodest before the LORD thy God in Horeb, when the LORD said unto me, Gather me the people together, and I will make them hear my words, that they may learn to fear me all the days that they shall live upon the earth, and that they may teach their children.*

## Misplacing God

How do people forget God? They forget God by *misplacing* God and *mislaying* God. As one author said, "To *mislay* God is to forget God." Another author said, "We build our skyscrapers and think we are safe. Everyone calls them skyscrapers except the sky. The sky looks at these puny things and does not call them skyscrapers." We magnify our efforts and forget the Lord. We substitute everything imaginable for the place we should give God in our life.

## Failure to Teach Our Children

God says, "This is my one and only way. There is no other way. You know Me in your heart and teach these things to your children. If you do not, you are forgetting Me."

The Bible says in Deuteronomy 6:4-7,

> *Hear, O Israel: The LORD our God is one LORD: and thou shalt love the LORD thy God with all thine heart, and with all thy soul, and with all thy might. And these*

123

> *words, which I command thee this day, shall be in thine heart: and thou shalt teach them diligently unto thy children, and shalt talk of them when thou sittest in thine house, and when thou walkest by the way, and when thou liest down, and when thou risest up.*

Deuteronomy 6:10-12 says,

> *And it shall be, when the LORD thy God shall have brought thee into the land which he sware unto thy fathers, to Abraham, to Isaac, and to Jacob, to give thee great and goodly cities, which thou buildedst not, and houses full of all good things, which thou filledst not, and wells digged, which thou diggedst not, vineyards and olive trees, which thou plantedst not; when thou shalt have eaten and be full; then beware lest thou forget the LORD, which brought thee forth out of the land of Egypt, from the house of bondage.*

God said, "When you get so blessed as a nation, beware. Your temptation is to forget your Maker. When you do not teach your children as I have commanded you, you have forgotten God."

## Failure to Keep His Commandments

Deuteronomy 8:11 says, *"Beware that thou forget not the LORD thy God, in not keeping his commandments, and his judgments, and his statutes, which I command thee this day."* How do we forget God? Again and again, God says, "it is possible to forget Him." We go through our religious routine, but we are not teaching the truth of God's Word to our children. We are forgetting God.

Do you realize what you are raising when you forget God in your home? As we forget God in our homes, we are raising a generation that will transgress God's Word and say that the Bible is not for us. We are raising a generation that will become a nation of idolaters.

We are raising a generation that will be religious, but will develop their own false religion. We are raising a generation that God will judge because their Maker has been forgotten.

Why is it that today we have fifty-two million school age children in America, and only two out of every ten teenagers ever attend any kind of church? About one-half the children who are elementary age never attend any kind of church. We have sown to the wind, and we are reaping a whirlwind because we have forgotten God.

God has been forgotten. How can He be remembered? It is the responsibility of parents to teach their children the things of God.

The Bible says in Deuteronomy 32:20, *"And he said, I will hide my face from them, I will see what their end shall be: for they are a very froward generation, children in whom is no faith."* What could possibly be more tragic than a generation of children in whom is no faith?

We are sowing the wind, and we will reap the whirlwind. If God did not spare His ancient people Israel, do you think that God will spare our country? We need to pray every day that God will send revival, and that it will begin in our hearts. We must start in our own homes to teach the truth to this generation.

# CHAPTER NINE
# WANDERERS AMONG THE NATIONS

e are listening to the heart of God as we listen to the heart of this prophet, Hosea. In the calamity that came upon God's people Israel, we must not miss the broken heart of God. We know that our God is a God of compassion. The same Saviour we see in tears, weeping over Jerusalem in the New Testament, is the same God that we read of in the ninth chapter of Hosea.

The Bible says in Hosea 9:1-17,

> *Rejoice not, O Israel, for joy, as other people: for thou hast gone a whoring from thy God, thou hast loved a reward upon every cornfloor. The floor and the winepress shall not feed them, and the new wine shall fail in her. They shall not dwell in the LORD's land; but Ephraim shall return to Egypt, and they shall eat unclean things in Assyria. They shall not offer wine offerings to the LORD, neither shall they be pleasing unto him: their sacrifices shall be unto them as the bread of mourners; all that eat thereof shall be*

polluted: for their bread for their soul shall not come into the house of the LORD.

What will ye do in the solemn day, and in the day of the feast of the LORD? For, lo, they are gone because of destruction: Egypt shall gather them up, Memphis shall bury them: the pleasant places for their silver, nettles shall possess them: thorns shall be in their tabernacles. The days of visitation are come, the days of recompence are come; Israel shall know it: the prophet is a fool, the spiritual man is mad, for the multitude of thine iniquity, and the great hatred.

The watchman of Ephraim was with my God: but the prophet is a snare of a fowler in all his ways, and hatred in the house of his God. They have deeply corrupted themselves, as in the days of Gibeah: therefore he will remember their iniquity, he will visit their sins. I found Israel like grapes in the wilderness; I saw your fathers as the firstripe in the fig tree at her first time: but they went to Baalpeor, and separated themselves unto that shame; and their abominations were according as they loved.

As for Ephraim, their glory shall fly away like a bird, from the birth, and from the womb, and from the conception. Though they bring up their children, yet will I bereave them, that there shall not be a man left: yea, woe also to them when I depart from them! Ephraim, as I saw Tyrus, is planted in a pleasant place: but Ephraim shall bring forth his children to the murderer. Give them, O LORD: what wilt thou give? give them a miscarrying womb and dry breasts.

128

*All their wickedness is in Gilgal: for there I hated them: for the wickedness of their doings I will drive them out of mine house, I will love them no more: all their princes are revolters. Ephraim is smitten, their root is dried up, they shall bear no fruit: yea, though they bring forth, yet will I slay even the beloved fruit of their womb. My God will cast them away, because they did not hearken unto him: and they shall be wanderers among the nations.*

The Lord says His people will become *"wanderers among the nations."* They are *"wanderers among the nations"* to this very hour. As you begin to read the Bible from the book of Genesis, traveling through the Word of God, you find that there is a God who loves His people. Not only does He love His people, but He makes promises to His people.

Israel is the nation that God raised up to whom and through whom He makes Himself known to the whole world. This is a principle that we are never to forget. It is not only *to* these people, but *through* these people that the Lord wants to make Himself known to the whole world. That same principle is in effect in the lives of believers today. Our God desires to make Himself known to His people so that through them, He will be made known to all others.

We find in Abraham a history of Israel beginning with God's call. The Bible says in Genesis 12:1-3,

*Now the LORD had said unto Abram, Get thee out of thy country, and from thy kindred, and from thy father's house, unto a land that I will shew thee: and I will make of thee a great nation, and I will bless thee, and make thy name great; and thou shalt be a blessing: and I will bless them that bless thee, and curse him that curseth thee: and in thee shall all families of the earth be blessed.*

God promised a child to Abraham and Sarah. That child was Isaac. God's covenant with Abraham was passed on from Isaac, to Jacob, to the sons of Jacob. After four hundred thirty years of bondage in Egypt, God raised up a people, a mighty nation. He delivered them out of bondage by the blood, through the Red Sea, and into their wilderness wanderings.

*In the calamity that came upon God's people Israel, we must not miss the broken heart of God. We know that our God is a God of compassion.*

After the death of Moses, Joshua led them across the Jordan River and into the land of promise. They conquered the enemy in the land of promise, divided the land, established a people, and chose a king. God brought them into that land, and now we arrive at the place in the book of Hosea where the prophet speaks about the people being removed from the land.

We read of all the Lord did to provide the land for His people, and now He is going to remove them from the land. Think of the sadness. What is to become of Israel?

The Bible says in Deuteronomy 7:6-11,

> *For thou art an holy people unto the LORD thy God: the LORD thy God hath chosen thee to be a special people unto himself, above all people that are upon the face of the earth. The LORD did not set his love upon you, nor choose you, because ye were more in number than any people; for ye were the fewest of all people: but because the LORD loved you, and because he would keep the oath which he had sworn unto your fathers, hath the LORD brought you out with a mighty hand, and redeemed you out of the house of*

*bondmen, from the hand of Pharaoh king of Egypt. Know therefore that the L*ORD *thy God, he is God, the faithful God, which keepeth covenant and mercy with them that love him and keep his commandments to a thousand generations; and repayeth them that hate him to their face, to destroy them: he will not be slack to him that hateth him, he will repay him to his face. Thou shalt therefore keep the commandments, and the statutes, and the judgments, which I command thee this day, to do them.*

I love the expression found in verse nine, *"the faithful God."* He is in all things *"the faithful God."*

The Bible says in Jeremiah 31:35-36,

*Thus saith the L*ORD*, which giveth the sun for a light by day, and the ordinances of the moon and of the stars for a light by night, which divideth the sea when the waves thereof roar; The L*ORD *of hosts is his name: if those ordinances depart from before me, saith the L*ORD*, then the seed of Israel also shall cease from being a nation before me for ever.*

God promised, "As long as there is a sun and a moon, and as long as the waves of the sea roar, the nation of Israel will exist." That is quite a promise, is it not?

Now the people are back in the land. On May 14, 1948 they were declared a nation. Eleven minutes after they declared their existence as a nation, the United States recognized them as the sovereign nation of Israel. In 1967 they regained possession of the old part of Jerusalem that they had longed for, and were able after the 1967 war to go to the Western Wall of the temple mount and offer their prayers. Ezekiel 36:24 says, *"For I will take you from among the*

131

*heathen, and gather you out of all countries, and will bring you into your own land."* He is doing this!

With all this in mind, think carefully about what Hosea 9:17 says, *"My God will cast them away, because they did not hearken unto him: and they shall be wanderers among the nations."* They would be wanderers. Because of unexplored territories, there were many people who thought in the dispersion of the northern kingdom that someone might eventually find a tremendously large group of Jews, all in one place. But after further exploration throughout the world, people realized that truly they were dispersed as *"wanderers among the nations."*

> *Any time you run from God, you are going in the wrong direction.*

We are reading in Hosea of events that happened centuries before the coming of Christ. For over 2,000 years, they were out of the land, and now they are back in the land. Many people believe this clock in prophecy is beginning to run again. They are back in blindness to the gospel; we have to keep that in mind. Take great interest in what God says here concerning these wanderers among the nations, God's chosen people, Israel.

## THE PUNISHMENT OF HIS PEOPLE

As we look at the punishment of Israel, I want you to think, "If God did not spare His own beloved people, what is ahead for sinning people today?" The Bible says in Hosea 9:1, *"Rejoice not, O Israel, for joy, as other people: for thou hast gone a whoring from thy God, thou hast loved a reward upon every cornfloor."* Evidently, the prophet is speaking to them in a time of a feast or celebration. He says, "Stop rejoicing!" He says, "As a people, you have turned from God, and all you want is what God will do for you. It is not the Lord you want; it is His reward. You want the blessing, but you never consider the God who provides all these blessings."

Hosea 9:2-3 says, *"The floor and the winepress shall not feed them, and the new wine shall fail in her. They shall not dwell in the* LORD*'s land; but Ephraim shall return to Egypt, and they shall eat unclean things in Assyria."* God has a land and a people for that land. But He said, "I am going to punish My people and remove them from the land."

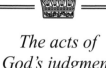

> The acts of God's judgment are acts of God's love

Verses four through six declare,

> *They shall not offer wine offerings to the* LORD, *neither shall they be pleasing unto him: their sacrifices shall be unto them as the bread of mourners; all that eat thereof shall be polluted: for their bread for their soul shall not come into the house of the* LORD. *What will ye do in the solemn day, and in the day of the feast of the* LORD? *For, lo, they are gone because of destruction: Egypt shall gather them up, Memphis shall bury them: the pleasant places for their silver, nettles shall possess them: thorns shall be in their tabernacles.*

When God's people got in trouble, they did not run to the Lord to escape their destruction; they ran to Egypt! The Bible says, "They ran from their destruction into destruction." They are going to be devoured there. Any time you run from God, you are going in the wrong direction.

When the Lord allows things to come upon us to deal with us and judge us, those things should get our attention and cause us to come to the Lord. The acts of God's judgment are acts of God's love just as much as Calvary was an act of God's love. They stop us in our tracks and cause us to rush to the Lord for His mercy.

Think about our beloved nation. Think twice before you think that nothing terrible could ever happen to us! If God would bring punishment upon His own dear people, Israel, He will not spare us when we are such a sinning people.

# THE PROOF OF GOD'S JUDGMENT

What evidence do we have for the judgment of God?

Hosea 9:7-13 says,

> *The days of visitation are come, the days of recompence are come; Israel shall know it: the prophet is a fool, the spiritual man is mad, for the multitude of thine iniquity, and the great hatred. The watchman of Ephraim was with my God: but the prophet is a snare of a fowler in all his ways, and hatred in the house of his God. They have deeply corrupted themselves, as in the days of Gibeah: therefore he will remember their iniquity, he will visit their sins. I found Israel like grapes in the wilderness; I saw your fathers as the firstripe in the fig tree at her first time: but they went to Baal-peor, and separated themselves unto that shame; and their abominations were according as they loved. As for Ephraim, their glory shall fly away like a bird, from the birth, and from the womb, and from the conception. Though they bring up their children, yet will I bereave them, that there shall not be a man left: yea, woe also to them when I depart from them! Ephraim, as I saw Tyrus, is planted in a pleasant place: but Ephraim shall bring forth his children to the murderer.*

134

If God's purpose for these people is to make Him known, why should they exist if they will not make Him known? All across America, there are churches diminishing and dying. When they are dying, they start trying to manufacture life with painted fire instead of praying for the Spirit of God to be upon them. Most start doing all they can to create activity, and activity is a poor substitute for spirituality. There are many busy churches with no spiritual life. We find ourselves wondering, "Why should they continue?"

God told the people, "You had such an opportunity, but now you are bringing your children to the murderer." God paints this word picture, saying, "There is no glory in your children's conception, there is no glory in the womb, and no glory in birth. If you have children, you are simply bringing them to the murderer."

What is becoming of the children of our nation? You can check the pulse of any nation by what they are doing with their children. In many places, we are raising them to have no knowledge of God, no faith, no holiness, and no decency.

I understand that this is a sad chapter, but the Lord is driving home a point concerning His people. It should be applied to all of us today.

# THE PRAYER OF THE PROPHET

What do we pray for in perilous times? How do you pray when you know that people are raising their children to deny God, and they are actually bringing their children to the murderer? The prayer of the prophet is found in verse fourteen.

First he prays, *"Give them, O LORD: what wilt thou give?"* It is as though he stops and pauses, not knowing what to ask. He says, "The more I think about them, the more I really do not know how to pray for them. What wilt Thou give?" Then he prays, *"Give them a*

135

*miscarrying womb and dry breasts."* Can you imagine the situation being so serious that the prophet prays, "It would be better for mothers not to give birth than to raise children to grow up and deny God. It would be better that they die in the womb than live to grow up, deny God, and go to hell forever." That is strong language, is it not? That is how he prayed. No wonder they called him a mad man. He certainly was not concerned with being politically correct!

> We must reseed our own land with the Word of God.

Listen to our country! Do you hear anything about God, decency, responsibility, morality, and accountability? There is an element that is so lost, so far removed from God, and so addicted to immorality. What kind of adults are they going to become? The prophet prayed, *"Give them a miscarrying womb and dry breasts."*

# THE PRONOUNCEMENT GOD MAKES CONCERNING HIS PEOPLE

The Lord uses a very special geographical location to make a solemn pronouncement. In Hosea 9:15 He says, *"All their wickedness is in Gilgal: for there I hated them: for the wickedness of their doings I will drive them out of mine house, I will love them no more: all their princes are revolters."*

Gilgal should have been a place remembered for the good things of God. Remember Joshua and the camp at Gilgal, and how God spoke to them there; it was a mighty place. In other words, when you walked around Gilgal, you should have been saying, "Glory to God! Do you remember how great God is? Think about what a heritage we have in Gilgal!" God says, "They are actually committing this terrible sin in Gilgal! They think nothing of their heritage! They sin in the presence of great blessing."

Thinking about our beloved nation, I wonder how many young people know our history, our founding fathers, and the blood, sweat, and tears that went into this country? I wonder if they know about Valley Forge, the price patriots paid, and their willingness to sacrifice? I wonder if this generation knows about any of our great heritage as a nation?

God said, "I watch them commit such sin in a place of such blessing." We need to stand against these revisionists who have rewritten the history of our country and taken God's favor out of it. We need to let children know about God's great hand on this country.

Israel began to die at the root. Hosea 9:16 says, *"Ephraim is smitten, their root is dried up, they shall bear no fruit: yea, though they bring forth, yet will I slay even the beloved fruit of their womb."* The Assyrians are coming to take them captive. They are going to cease to exist in the land. The northern kingdom, Israel, is going to be removed, and they are going to stay out of the land for more than 2,000 years. They have dishonored God, and God has removed His hand of blessing from them. After all the effort to get there, now they are going to be removed.

*You can check the pulse of any nation by what they are doing with their children.*

The Bible says in Hosea 9:17, *"My God will cast them away, because they did not hearken unto him: and they shall be wanderers among the nations."* Notice that little word *"because."* God makes it very simple. He says, "I did all this to them because they did not hearken unto Me."

I think about my country and the fact that we are not giving to our children and grandchildren the same nation that was given to us. So much is missing! A faith that has no fire and a Christian witness that has no power is going to be easily overtaken. We need our fire again! We need to be stirred up for God again! We need a wholehearted, Holy Ghost-empowered crusade to reach the children of America again. We must reseed our own land with the Word of God.

When traveling to England, I often fly into Birmingham. Much of our Christian heritage started in greater Birmingham, but now there is an Islamic section in that city where they are allowing Islamic law to be enacted instead of the full laws of Parliament. It is the most densely populated area of Islamic invasion in all of England.

*A faith that has no fire and a Christian witness that has no power is going to be easily overtaken. We need our fire again! We need to be stirred up for God again!*

Someone may ask, "How did that happen?" When families and churches who said they were Christians went to sleep, the enemy came in and took over. It is only the aggressive people who are advancing. Churches that will dare to be called foolish and will take a stand, and families who will be bold about their convictions can make that advance. There is ground to be taken! You do not take that ground passively.

Matthew 11:12 says, *"The kingdom of heaven suffereth violence, and the violent take it by force."* This means that we are in an army. We must be on the advance and do that which God has given us to do.

I want to take America back! I want our children and families back! I intend to raise my voice against what is wrong and do everything I can do to make it right. May God help us not to die before we die!

138

# AN EMPTY VINE

 eople and nations fail when they live for lesser things than God's glory. There is nothing so empty as the life that is given entirely for self-fulfillment. We are created by God for His purpose and His glory. Hosea chapter ten brings us to what should have and could have been in the lives of God's people. The Bible says in Hosea 10:1-15,

*Israel is an empty vine, he bringeth forth fruit unto himself: according to the multitude of his fruit he hath increased the altars; according to the goodness of his land they have made goodly images. Their heart is divided; now shall they be found faulty: he shall break down their altars, he shall spoil their images. For now they shall say, We have no king, because we feared not the LORD; what then should a king do to us? They have spoken words, swearing falsely in making a covenant: thus judgment springeth up as hemlock in the furrows of the field.*

*The inhabitants of Samaria shall fear because of
the calves of Beth-aven: for the people thereof shall
mourn over it, and the priests thereof that rejoiced on
it, for the glory thereof, because it is departed from it.
It shall be also carried unto Assyria for a present to
king Jareb: Ephraim shall receive shame, and Israel
shall be ashamed of his own counsel. As for Samaria,
her king is cut off as the foam upon the water. The
high places also of Aven, the sin of Israel, shall be
destroyed: the thorn and the thistle shall come up
on their altars; and they shall say to the mountains,
Cover us; and to the hills, Fall on us.*

*O Israel, thou hast sinned from the days of Gibeah:
there they stood: the battle in Gibeah against the
children of iniquity did not overtake them. It is in
my desire that I should chastise them; and the people
shall be gathered against them, when they shall bind
themselves in their two furrows. And Ephraim is as
an heifer that is taught, and loveth to tread out the
corn; but I passed over upon her fair neck: I will
make Ephraim to ride; Judah shall plow, and Jacob
shall break his clods.*

*Sow to yourselves in righteousness, reap in mercy;
break up your fallow ground: for it is time to seek the
LORD, till he come and rain righteousness upon you.
Ye have plowed wickedness, ye have reaped iniquity;
ye have eaten the fruit of lies: because thou didst
trust in thy way, in the multitude of thy mighty men.
Therefore shall a tumult arise among thy people, and
all thy fortresses shall be spoiled, as Shalman spoiled
Beth-arbel in the day of battle: the mother was
dashed in pieces upon her children. So shall Beth-el*

*do unto you because of your great wickedness: in a
morning shall the king of Israel utterly be cut off.*

*"Israel is an empty vine."* The word picture is that of a flowing
vine with every appearance of life and fruitfulness. After divine
examination, the fruit God intended for that vine is not found on it.

Many Bible students make the mistake of reading Old Testament
passages in the word of God and thinking that it has absolutely
nothing to do with them. This passage may be directed by the Lord
to Israel, but it is intended for all of God's people. There are many
things that God deals with in this chapter, giving somewhat of a
summary of His judgment upon His people.

## GOD PLANTED A VINEYARD
## FOR ALL PEOPLE

The heart of our God is a missionary heart. It is our Lord's
intention to make Himself known to Israel and through them, make
Himself known to the whole world. Any time a group of people has
the idea that they are the only people for which God intended His
grace and mercy, they have misunderstood the heart of God.

The Lord says that Israel is an empty vine. It is possible to
prostitute the resources that God gives us by consuming them on
ourselves. All through the Scriptures God speaks of His people
Israel as a vine. The Bible says in Isaiah 5:1-2,

> *Now will I sing to my well-beloved a song of my
> beloved touching his vineyard. My well-beloved hath
> a vineyard in a very fruitful hill: and he fenced it, and
> gathered out the stones thereof, and planted it with
> the choicest vine, and built a tower in the midst of it,
> and also made a winepress therein: and he looked*

*that it should bring forth grapes, and it brought forth wild grapes.*

It brought forth fruit, but not the fruit God intended. There was energy expended, but not the emphasis God intended. There was labor put forth, but not where God intended it to be put forth. In the eyes of God, it is an empty vine. It does not have the fruit God intended it to have.

The Bible says in Isaiah 5:3-4, *"And now, O inhabitants of Jerusalem, and men of Judah, judge, I pray you, betwixt me and my vineyard. What could have been done more to my vineyard, that I have not done in it?"*

The Lord provided every blessing it needed to flourish. Every resource necessary for the right growth, God had given. But His blessings had been misappropriated. They were consumed in this world and for this world.

God planted a vineyard to be a blessing to all people. The Bible says in Hosea 10:1, *"Israel is an empty vine, he bringeth forth fruit unto himself: according to the multitude of his fruit he hath increased the altars; according to the goodness of his land they have made goodly images."*

*"He bringeth forth fruit unto himself."* All has been consumed upon himself. The Bible also says, *"He hath increased the altars."* The altars did not increase this empty vine; the empty vine increased the altars. The more he had, the more altars he constructed. These certainly were not altars to the true and living God.

The Bible says that he made goodly or artistic images. He fashioned these things with his hand. He made them as beautiful as possible because in his eyes, they were the things that held the most beauty. In the eyes of God, what is most beautiful? The wounds of the Saviour, who bled and died and paid our sin debt, are most beautiful in the eyes of God. He shed His own blood that we might be made clean.

During the days of Nazism in Germany, churches either had to capitulate and conform to what the Nazis said or resist and follow the Scriptures, knowing they would be persecuted for their resistance. We are not living in Nazi Germany, but the world is pressuring God's people, and many of God's people are bowing to that pressure. Churches either bow to that pressure and please the world, or they yield more and more to the Bible.

Are we ashamed to bear the blood-stained banner of the Lord Jesus Christ? Do we stand true for God? We have a vine, but is it an empty vine? We are to bear the fruit that God intended.

> *People and nations fail when they live for lesser things than God's glory.*

The Bible says in verse two, *"Their heart is divided."* Remember the prophet Elijah standing before the people and King Ahab? He said, *"How long halt ye between two opinions?"* (I Kings 18:21). So many have a heart divided between two opinions.

Do you remember how this book of the Bible started with the tragic story of Hosea and his marriage to Gomer? It began with her betrayal of his love. The Bible story we are reading started with the home life of Hosea and Gomer and her divided heart. Sure, she had some feelings for Hosea, but she had other lovers.

I have a lovely wife who has been my faithful companion since 1967. Can you imagine me saying of my wife, "This is *one* of the women I really love"? How long do you think she would put up with that?

That is the way we treat our God. We give Him a place alongside others. We indicate we have affection for Him, and others…and

others…and others. God's Word says of ancient Israel, *"Their heart is divided."*

Hosea 10:2-3 says, *"Their heart is divided; now shall they be found faulty: he shall break down their altars, he shall spoil their images. For now they shall say, We have no king, because we feared not the LORD; what then should a king do to us?"* This is their sad lament. Remember, all they wanted was a king like other nations.

# WE ARE ACCOUNTABLE TO GOD FOR EVERY BENEFIT THAT IS OURS

Every benefit deposited in our lives brings with it greater accountability to God. Why has God blessed us? Why did God bless Israel? He has not given us His blessings so we can consume them on ourselves. The things God has blessed and benefited us with are things that God intends for us to use for His glory, and we are accountable to Him for them.

> *It is possible to prostitute the resources that God gives us by consuming them on ourselves.*

We are considering the Lord's vine. One article I read said that a vine like this should not be allowed to bear fruit for three years. The horticulturist said the vine should be pruned, cut, and strengthened, and after three years allowed to bear fruit. Think of this pruning and strengthening as it relates to our lives.

There are times in our lives when we wonder, "Is the fruit going to come?" If we are living in obedience to God, it will come. Let us recognize our accountability to the Lord.

The Bible says in John 15:1-5,

*I am the true vine, and my Father is the husbandman. Every branch in me that beareth not fruit he taketh away: and every branch that beareth fruit, he purgeth it, that it may bring forth more fruit. Now ye are clean through the word which I have spoken unto you. Abide in me, and I in you. As the branch cannot bear fruit of itself, except it abide in the vine; no more can ye, except ye abide in me. I am the vine, ye are the branches: he that abideth in me, and I in him, the same bringeth forth much fruit: for without me ye can do nothing.*

Everything that comes to us as a branch is coming from our God. He is the vine; we are the branches. These benefits that are ours are coming from our God. Why has God given to me the responsibilities and opportunities He has? Why has God brought into my life certain people to influence me? There is nothing in my life that can be counted as a benefit that I shall not give God an account of how I used it.

That is what the Lord declares to His people. The Bible says in Hosea 10:4-5,

*They have spoken words, swearing falsely in making a covenant: thus judgment springeth up as hemlock in the furrows of the field. The inhabitants of Samaria shall fear because of the calves of Beth-aven: for the people thereof shall mourn over it, and the priests thereof that rejoiced on it, for the glory thereof, because it is departed from it.*

Can you imagine God's people finding golden images before which to bow down? They were not mourning over the loss of their land or their sin; they were not weeping because of their iniquity. They were upset because their idols were gone! They used God's

147

blessings falsely to produce these things for themselves, and now that their images are gone, they are weeping. How we respond to God determines how God deals with us.

Hosea 10:6-8 says,

> *It shall be also carried unto Assyria for a present to king Jareb: Ephraim shall receive shame, and Israel shall be ashamed of his own counsel. As for Samaria, her king is cut off as the foam upon the water. The high places also of Aven, the sin of Israel, shall be destroyed: the thorn and the thistle shall come up on their altars; and they shall say to the mountains, Cover us; and to the hills, Fall on us.*

What could have been a place of beauty and continued glory to God was now covered in ruins. All across our land there are those who had the opportunity to do God's work God's way but did not, and now nothing is left. Many families once had the opportunity to serve and honor the Lord but did not, and there is now nothing left. God holds us accountable.

# WE ARE GOING TO REAP WHAT WE SOW

The record of our sins is recorded by the Lord until it is confessed and forsaken. The Word of God says in Hosea 10:9, *"O Israel, thou hast sinned from the days of Gibeah: there they stood: the battle in Gibeah against the children of iniquity did not overtake them."* God kept up with their unconfessed sins. They could have had them removed by confessing them and seeking the Lord.

There are sinfully low events which stand out. They exemplify how low people have gone. This is illustrated in an event in the book of Judges. The Bible says in Judges 19:17-30,

> *And when he had lifted up his eyes, he saw a wayfaring man in the street of the city: and the old man said, Whither goest thou? and whence comest thou? And he said unto him, We are passing from Bethlehem-judah toward the side of mount Ephraim; from thence am I: and I went to Bethlehem-judah, but I am now going to the house of the LORD; and there is no man that receiveth me to house. Yet there is both straw and provender for our asses; and there is bread and wine also for me, and for thy handmaid, and for the young man which is with thy servants: there is no want of any thing. And the old man said, Peace be with thee; howsoever let all thy wants lie upon me; only lodge not in the street. So he brought him into his house, and gave provender unto the asses: and they washed their feet, and did eat and drink.*

> *Now as they were making their hearts merry, behold, the men of the city, certain sons of Belial, beset the house round about, and beat at the door, and spake to the master of the house, the old man, saying, Bring forth the man that came into thine house, that we may know him. And the man, the master of the house, went out unto them, and said unto them, Nay, my brethren, nay, I pray you, do not so wickedly; seeing that this man is come into mine house, do not this folly. Behold, here is my daughter a maiden, and his concubine; them I will bring out now, and humble ye them, and do with them what seemeth good unto you: but unto this man do not so vile a thing.*

149

*But the men would not hearken to him: so the man took his concubine, and brought her forth unto them; and they knew her, and abused her all the night until the morning: and when the day began to spring, they let her go. Then came the woman in the dawning of the day, and fell down at the door of the man's house where her lord was, till it was light. And her lord rose up in the morning, and opened the doors of the house, and went out to go his way: and, behold, the woman his concubine was fallen down at the door of the house, and her hands were upon the threshold. And he said unto her, Up, and let us be going. But none answered. Then the man took her up upon an ass, and the man rose up, and gat him unto his place.*

*And when he was come into his house, he took a knife, and laid hold on his concubine, and divided her, together with her bones, into twelve pieces, and sent her into all the coasts of Israel. And it was so, that all that saw it said, There was no such deed done nor seen from the day that the children of Israel came up out of the land of Egypt unto this day: consider of it, take advice, and speak your minds.*

This so enraged the men that they gathered a mighty force and nearly wiped out the entire tribe of Benjamin. Why does God call attention to things like this? There are events and moments in life that mark how terrible sin is in our land.

In Deuteronomy 28:63 we read, *"And it shall come to pass, that as the LORD rejoiced over you to do you good, and to multiply you; so the LORD will rejoice over you to destroy you, and to bring you to nought; and ye shall be plucked from off the land whither thou goest to possess it."* The Lord declares that with the same desire He desired

to bless the people, He would with that same desire *"rejoice over you to destroy you."*

Hosea 10:11 says, *"And Ephraim is as an heifer that is taught, and loveth to tread out the corn; but I passed over upon her fair neck: I will make Ephraim to ride; Judah shall plow, and Jacob shall break his clods."* Here the Lord gives a picture of an animal loving to do what it does. He says, "That is the way you have been. You have done as you pleased. But you have not been made to plough. You have enjoyed the blessed benefit without ever considering the ploughing. You did not know where the blessings came from; but you are going to learn now." We are all guilty of taking God's blessings for granted. This means, of course, that we take God for granted.

*Every benefit deposited in our lives brings with it greater accountability to God.*

It is the Lord's desire to bless His people. The Bible says in Hosea 10:12, *"Sow to yourselves in righteousness, reap in mercy; break up your fallow ground: for it is time to seek the LORD, till he come and rain righteousness upon you."*

Instead of blessing, the Lord makes the strongest indictment against His people. The Bible says in Hosea 10:13-14,

> *Ye have plowed wickedness, ye have reaped iniquity; ye have eaten the fruit of lies: because thou didst trust in thy way, in the multitude of thy mighty men. Therefore shall a tumult arise among thy people, and all thy fortresses shall be spoiled, as Shalman spoiled Beth-arbel in the day of battle: the mother was dashed in pieces upon her children.*

The Lord gives an example of an Assyrian king destroying a city. He tells how terrible it was, saying, *"The mother was dashed in pieces upon her children."* Tragic events highlight God's judgment. Do you think of examples of tragic times in your life? Do you remember times of tragedy when you made promises to God? May God bring back to our minds the promises we made to Him when we were moved in our hearts and stirred to do what He wanted us to do. The Lord has a way of reminding us.

*All across our land there are those who had the opportunity to do God's work God's way but did not, and now nothing is left.*

The Bible says in Hosea 10:15, *"So shall Beth-el do unto you because of your great wickedness: in a morning shall the king of Israel utterly be cut off."* Have we had time to repent? The final blow of judgment will fall. When it does, we will all know we waited until it was too late.

Has God given us time? Have we used it wisely? Has God given us health? Can that health be removed? Has God given us children? Have we given them to Christ? Are we putting into their lives things that are eternal?

We are busy! We are as a vine spread everywhere. But God examines the fruit. Are we bearing the fruit God intended to be on the vine?

# CHAPTER ELEVEN

# I LOVED HIM

Weak Christians cannot help a needy world. We live in a world of ever increasing need, and we must be strong in the Lord if we are going to have the right effect on this needy world.

The gospel message is the message we are to take to all people. The Lord Jesus said He came to seek and to save that which was lost (Luke 19:10). The message of the book of Hosea is the message of the gospel. He seeks and saves.

We must be strong in the Lord—and especially strong in the love of God. We move now into Hosea chapter eleven. Hosea 11:1-12

> *When Israel was a child, then I loved him, and called my son out of Egypt. As they called them, so they went from them: they sacrificed unto Baalim, and burned incense to graven images. I taught Ephraim also to go, taking them by their arms; but they knew not that I healed them. I drew them with cords of a man, with bands of love: and I was to them*

155

*as they that take off the yoke on their jaws, and I laid meat unto them.*

*He shall not return into the land of Egypt, but the Assyrian shall be his king, because they refused to return. And the sword shall abide on his cities, and shall consume his branches, and devour them, because of their own counsels. And my people are bent to backsliding from me: though they called them to the most High, none at all would exalt him.*

*How shall I give thee up, Ephraim? How shall I deliver thee, Israel? how shall I make thee as Admah? how shall I set thee as Zeboim? mine heart is turned within me, my repentings are kindled together. I will not execute the fierceness of mine anger, I will not return to destroy Ephraim: for I am God, and not man; the Holy One in the midst of thee: and I will not enter into the city.*

*They shall walk after the LORD: he shall roar like a lion: when he shall roar, then the children shall tremble from the west. They shall tremble as a bird out of Egypt, and as a dove out of the land of Assyria: and I will place them in their houses, saith the LORD. Ephraim compasseth me about with lies, and the house of Israel with deceit: but Judah yet ruleth with God, and is faithful with the saints.*

With extreme tenderness, the Lord says in verse one, *"When Israel was a child, then I loved him."* Looking into the faces of children causes us to contemplate what great things can be done with life. Too often, at the end of life, we are only thinking of what could have been. What promise there was when Israel was a child, loved of God!

This glimpse of God's love in the eleventh chapter of Hosea brings us near the conclusion of the book. The last four chapters of Hosea deal with this same subject of God's love. Do not forget how God opened this story to us with the life of Hosea, Gomer, and the children.

Remember those children. Remember when the last child came, there was no doubt that it was not Hosea's child. Hosea loved his wife Gomer. They had a marriage that evidently began in the right way, and then doubts came and sin entered in. Finally, Hosea is seen going through the streets of the city, seeking for Gomer, finding her as a slave, and buying her back unto himself.

*We live in a world of ever increasing need, and we must be strong in the Lord if we are going to have the right effect on this needy world.*

In that story, God tells us the story of our lives, of our salvation, and most importantly, of His great love for us. From the slave market of sin, He purchased us to be His very own. This is also the story of Israel and of God's great love for them. It tells how He dealt with His chosen people. So many important lessons can be learned from God's love.

# THE CHILD OF GOD'S LOVE

We read how tenderly God tells this story. He says, *"When Israel was a child, then I loved him, and called my son out of Egypt."* Of course, the Lord is not saying that this is the only time He loved him; but He is emphasizing the love He had for Israel, as a father would love a child, calling him out of Egypt.

Of course, a prophetic message is seen here. The Lord Jesus Christ would come out of Egypt; but remember that God's people

were in Egyptian bondage, and He brought them out. Their yoke was broken through the deliverance by the blood. In this chapter, the Lord speaks as a father would talk to a small child.

> Let us consider how our rebellion affects our God.

Circle the pronoun *"I"* in verse one. Then notice beginning in verse three, *"I taught Ephraim...I healed them...I drew them...I laid meat unto them."* The Lord speaks as a tender, compassionate father speaking to his child, saying, *"I loved him, and called my son out of Egypt. As they called them, so they went from them: they sacrificed unto Baalim, and burned incense to graven images."* He said "I watched my son turn to these graven images, to Baalim and idolatry." He recalls, *"I taught Ephraim also."*

If you are a parent, then you remember as a father or mother the devotion you gave to your children. You loved them and taught them. God expresses, *"I taught Ephraim also to go, taking them by their arms."* My wife and I can remember when our boys came along, and they started crawling around. One of us would take them by the arms, and the other would get just a short distance away. We would lead them by the arms until they could take a step on their own.

No doubt parents have done that for all time. God says, "I remember you; I remember you like a precious child!" He treated them like a father who would take his small child in his arms and take keenest delight in holding him by the arms, helping him to walk.

*"But they knew not that I healed them."* The children were sick and needy, and the Lord healed them. He said, *"I drew them with cords of a man, with bands of love."* These are expressions of love. He goes on to say. *"I was to them as they that take off the yoke."* He speaks now as a herdsman saying, "As a man who cares for an animal

that has been working all day and comes to be relieved of its burden, I have cared for you with loving tenderness, removing your yoke."

The Lord came to us. He sought us by His blessed Spirit; He redeemed us by His precious blood. He held us like a precious child and taught us how to walk. He fed us, healed us, and eased our burden at the end of the day. As Hosea pens these words, no doubt he thinks of how he loves his own children and wife, and he is reminded of Israel.

# THE CONFLICT OF GOD'S LOVE

Every parent will understand exactly what we read in this passage. The Bible says in verse five. *"He shall not return into the land of Egypt, but the Assyrian shall be his king, because they refused to return."*

God, as a Father, was able to know the direction of His children's lives. He knew where they were headed. He knew the cruel Assyrians would rule over them. The Bible says, *"And the sword shall abide on his cities, and shall consume his branches, and devour them, because of their own counsels."* He says, *"And my people are bent to backsliding."* They were going to be consumed; their cities were going to be destroyed. Their *"branches,"* their mighty men, were going to be devoured because of their own counsel. They would not heed God's counsel.

Any father who loves a child and has seen that child go in the wrong direction, headed toward destruction, has felt something of what God is telling us here. *"And my people are bent to backsliding from me: though they called them to the most High, none at all would exalt him."* They have called to the Most High, yet they are going to be servants of an Assyrian king.

Our Lord opens up His great heart to tell us of His suffering, His grief, and His conflict. He asks these questions. *"How shall I give thee up, Ephraim? how shall I deliver thee, Israel? How shall I make*

*thee as Admah? how shall I set thee as Zeboim? mine heart is turned within me, my repentings are kindled together."* God says, "How can I bear this? I have loved you so! I have fed you and healed you; I relieved your burdens. I have called you, and now I see where you are headed." His great heart *"is turned within."*

Instead of living in fellowship with their God, they chose the abuse of an Assyrian king. With a broken heart, the Lord asked, *"How shall I give thee up?"* Let us consider how our rebellion affects our God.

This is the conflict of God's love. He mentions two cities in this text. In verse eight, he reminds the people of Admah and Zeboim. In Genesis 14:2, the Lord mentions these cities and their kings near Sodom and Gomorrah. The beautiful place God established for His people will become as Admah and Zeboim. This act of God's judgment turned His heart within Him.

## THE CONCLUSION OF GOD'S LOVE

Read with great care what the Lord says in verse nine concerning what He will not do and why He will not do it, *"I will not execute the fierceness of mine anger, I will not return to destroy Ephraim: for I am God, and not man; the Holy One in the midst of thee: and I will not enter into the city."*

In Egypt, He came and wanted the people. In Sodom and Gomorra, He said, "I am not coming into the city." How could God look at this sinful, wayward people about to be carried away by the Assyrians and declare, *"I will not execute the fierceness of mine anger, I will not return to destroy Ephraim: for I am God, and not man."*

The Lord tells us in Romans 3:26, *"To declare, I say, at this time his righteousness: that he might be just."* Is God just—yes or no?

Yes! If He is a just God, then sin must be punished. If His children are worshiping Baalim and building images of idols, what will He do?

Again, the Bible says in Romans 3:26, *"To declare, I say, at this time his righteousness: that he might be just, and the justifier of him which believeth in Jesus."* This is the conclusion of God's love, the ultimate climax. This is the most beautiful picture of God's love because the Lord declares the fact that He is God, and not man. He punishes sin yet forgives sinners.

The Bible says, *"For God so loved the world, that he gave his only begotten Son, that whosoever believeth in him should not perish, but have everlasting life"* (John 3:16). We should go to hell for our sin. Every man that has ever lived should go to hell for his sin. But God sent

> *God is just because the debt has been paid. He is the Justifier because His dear Son, the Lord Jesus, paid the debt.*

His only begotten Son to bleed and die and suffer our hell for us. He paid the debt we owed. God is just because the debt has been paid. He is the Justifier because His dear Son, the Lord Jesus, paid the debt.

Let us go back to Hosea chapter eleven. The Lord immediately speaks of another day. He lifts our minds to another day, another hour for Israel. The people are going into captivity, but He says in verse ten, *"They shall walk after the Lord."* When will they *"walk after the Lord"*? We see the answer as we read on.

*"He shall roar like a lion: when he shall roar, then the children shall tremble from the west."* This is a prophetic message concerning Israel and the west. *"They shall tremble as a bird out of Egypt, and as a dove out of the land of Assyria: and I will place them in their houses, saith the Lord."* Each of the pictures is a prophetic message.

This sounds much like what the Lord Jesus said in John 14:1-6,

*Let not your heart be troubled: ye believe in God, believe also in me. In my Father's house are many mansions: if it were not so, I would have told you. I go to prepare a place for you. And if I go and prepare a place for you, I will come again, and receive you unto myself; that where I am, there ye may be also. And whither I go ye know, and the way ye know. Thomas saith unto him, Lord, we know not whither thou goest; and how can we know the way? Jesus saith unto him, I am the way, the truth, and the life: no man cometh unto the Father, but by me.*

In the days of Hosea, as God's people were about to be taken captive, the Lord knew that Christ was coming to pay the awful price of sin that a holy God demanded, and that someday Israel could live again the way God intended. Jesus Christ's death, burial, and resurrection provides the way to God.

Through Hosea, the Lord gives this amazing declaration, *"Ephraim compasseth me about with lies, and the house of Israel with deceit: but Judah yet ruleth with God, and is faithful with the saints."*

The Lord takes this chapter, buried deeply in the Old Testament, written seven hundred years before the coming of Christ, and gives us a glimpse of things to come. It is a glimpse of God's love. He pictured Israel as a child. His heart is vexed and troubled—"How can I? How can I? How can I?" What is the conclusion of His love? "I am going to spare these people!" The reason they can be spared is because the sin debt will be justly paid by the Lord Jesus Christ.

Put yourself in this passage. See again that God loves you. Witness the conflict of God's suffering heart—grieved when you do not obey Him like you ought to obey Him. View by faith the conclusion of God's love, that He paid your debt on Calvary and made a way that you can come to Him for forgiveness and cleansing and be made whole.

CHAPTER TWELVE

# FEEDING ON THE WIND

 wise man once said to me that the only purpose some people serve is to provide a bad example. Those people's lives speak loudly about what we are not to do.

Those who feed on the wind learn that their appetite is never satisfied. The nation of Israel fed on the wind. The east wind that blew across the Arabian Desert into the land of Israel was a wind of desolation and destruction.

The Lord tells us of the deceitful appetite of His wayward people in Hosea 12:1-14. God says,

> *Ephraim feedeth on wind, and followeth after the east wind: he daily increaseth lies and desolation; and they do make a covenant with the Assyrians, and oil is carried into Egypt. The LORD hath also a controversy with Judah, and will punish Jacob according to his ways; according to his doings will he recompense him. He took his brother by the heel in the womb, and by his strength he had power with*

165

*God: yea, he had power over the angel, and prevailed: he wept, and made supplication unto him: he found him in Beth-el, and there he spake with us; even the LORD God of hosts; the LORD is his memorial.*

*Therefore turn thou to thy God: keep mercy and judgment, and wait on thy God continually. He is a merchant, the balances of deceit are in his hand: he loveth to oppress. And Ephraim said, Yet I am become rich, I have found me out substance: in all my labours they shall find none iniquity in me that were sin. And I that am the LORD thy God from the land of Egypt will yet make thee to dwell in tabernacles, as in the days of the solemn feast. I have also spoken by the prophets, and I have multiplied visions, and used similitudes, by the ministry of the prophets.*

*Is there iniquity in Gilead? surely they are vanity: they sacrifice bullocks in Gilgal; yea, their altars are as heaps in the furrows of the fields. And Jacob fled into the country of Syria, and Israel served for a wife, and for a wife he kept sheep. And by a prophet the LORD brought Israel out of Egypt, and by a prophet was he preserved. Ephraim provoked him to anger most bitterly: therefore shall he leave his blood upon him, and his reproach shall his Lord return unto him.*

Ephraim *"feedeth on"* and *"followeth after"* the wind. The Lord is our true nourishment. We are to feed on Christ. The Lord Jesus is our bread and our water.

We live in a world filled with people who are feeding on the wind. Not only do they feed on the wind, once they get a taste of that east wind, they follow after it; they want more of the wind.

166

The Bible says in Hosea 12:1, *"He daily increaseth lies and desolation."* Nothing remains the same. If we feed on the Lord, we shall want more of the Lord. If we feed on the wind, we shall want more of the wind. Do you have an appetite for God or for the things of this world? Wherever you have cultivated an appetite, it will increase and you will want more. If you are feeding on the wind of this world, you will want more of that. If you are feeding on the Lord, you will want more of Him. May God help us to understand and apply this truth.

The Lord Jesus Christ said in John 6:26-35,

> *Verily, verily, I say unto you, Ye seek me, not because ye saw the miracles, but because ye did eat of the loaves, and were filled. Labour not for the meat which perisheth, but for that meat which endureth unto everlasting life, which the Son of man shall give unto you: for him hath God the Father sealed. Then said they unto him, What shall we do, that we might work the works of God? Jesus answered and said unto them, This is the work of God, that ye believe on him whom he hath sent. They said therefore unto him, What sign shewest thou then, that we may see, and believe thee? what dost thou work? Our fathers did eat manna in the desert; as it is written, He gave them bread from heaven to eat. Then Jesus said unto them, Verily, verily, I say unto you, Moses gave you not that bread from heaven; but my Father giveth you the true bread from heaven. For the bread of God is he which cometh down from heaven, and giveth life unto the world. Then said they unto him, Lord, evermore give us this bread. And Jesus said unto them, I am the bread of life: he that cometh to me shall never hunger; and he that believeth on me shall never thirst.*

# THE MEMORIAL OF THE LORD

The Bible says in Hosea 12:5, *"Even the LORD God of hosts; the LORD is his memorial."* Note the phrase, *"The LORD is his memorial."* This is the strong point that God is making to His prophet.

*If we feed on the Lord, we shall want more of the Lord. If we feed on the wind, we shall want more of the wind. Do you have an appetite for God or for the things of this world?*

Remember in verse one He stated, *"Ephraim feedeth on wind, and followeth after the east wind: he daily increaseth lies and desolation."* With every passing day it grew worse. The Bible continues in verse one, *"and they do make a covenant with the Assyrians."* The people ran to the Assyrians for help, and God is going to allow the very people that they have turned to for help to take them into captivity. There is a spiritual lesson for all of us here. The lesson is that the thing that we go after, that we want more of, that we depend upon, that we think serves us, soon becomes our master. The people of Israel said, "We are going to ask the Assyrians to aid us." It did not take long until the Assyrians were no longer their helpers, but their masters.

Verse one continues saying, *"oil is carried into Egypt."* Oil was the most precious commodity in Israel. To appease the Egyptians, they took the most precious commodity they had in their land, olive oil in this case, and made it a gift to the Egyptians. How many people have offered the most precious thing God has given them to this unbelieving world?

The Bible says in Hosea 12:2, *"The LORD hath also a controversy with Judah, and will punish Jacob according to his ways; according*

168

*to his doings will he recompense him."* Now the Lord speaks of the two tribes to the south. The Lord says He is going to deal with Jacob.

Hosea 12:3 says, *"He took his brother by the heel in the womb, and by his strength he had power with God."* The reference is of course to the birth of Jacob and Esau. If you remember, Jacob and Esau were in the same womb. Esau was coming out first, but Jacob came with his hand on the heel of his brother. They gave him the name Jacob which means "a heel grabber" or "a deceiver."

God declares again that He was there when Jacob was born. The Lord says in Hosea 12:3-4, *"He took his brother by the heel in the womb, and by his strength he had power with God: yea, he had power over the angel, and prevailed: he wept, and made supplication unto him."* He speaks here of Jacob's two events in Beth-el, the house of God. Jacob prevailed and wept. Even in the writings of Moses, God does not tell us about Jacob weeping; but here, in Hosea 12:4, He tells us that Jacob was in such desperation that he wept.

Hosea asked, "Can you remember how God dealt with Jacob?" He speaks collectively here about the tribes of Israel. Jacob's name was changed to Israel. Hosea states, "I want you to think about something. God wants you to think about your history—how He found you, how He raised you up, and how He made a mighty nation out of you. I want you to think about when your father Jacob prayed and made a covenant with God. I want you to think about how God blessed him, protected him, and delivered him. Think about all these things."

The Bible says in Hosea 12:5, *"Even the LORD God of hosts; the LORD is his memorial."* What does this mean? It means the Lord of hosts, the God of the visible and the invisible, is to be your memorial. When you remember God, you are not to remember places, things, or blessings; you are to remember where they came from. Remember that it is God who gave you all of this. This is the way God's people are to think. *"The LORD is his memorial."*

169

We read in Exodus chapter three of Moses seeking to know more of the Lord. Exodus 3:13 says, *"And Moses said unto God, Behold, when I come unto the children of Israel, and shall say unto them, The God of your fathers hath sent me unto you; and they shall say to me, What is his name? what shall I say unto them?"*

God answered Moses' question in Exodus 3:14, *"And God said unto Moses, I AM THAT I AM: and he said, Thus shalt thou say unto the children of Israel, I AM hath sent me unto you."* In other words, God said He should always be remembered as the great *"I AM."* This is the memorial of the Lord, the way we remember the Lord, and the way we refer to the Lord. He is always the God of the present. He is always the God who is the great *"I AM."* He is the eternally present God. We may speak of the Lord as being the same yesterday, today, and forever. Our reference may be to the past, present, or future, but God has no past or future. He is the eternally present One.

As we consider our lives, let us move our thinking from ancient Israel to this moment in time. How is God memorialized in our thinking? When you think of the Lord, is He a God only of the past? No, but many speak only about God in the past. I hear many speak only of what God has done. God never wants to be remembered as the God of the past only. He is not the God who said, "I WAS." He said, *"I AM."*

These people had a great heritage, but that is all they had. Any time a church or an individual Christian allows God to become only their heritage, they are finished. What is He to us in the present moment? These people could say, "We know the God of Abraham, and the God of Isaac, and the God of Jacob. We can tell you wonderful things that God has done in the past." Is He the God of this present moment in your life? The memorial of the Lord is that He is always the God who is the "I AM." Dear friends, we can be grateful for our heritage, but we must always live the Christian life in the present. God must be real to us at this moment.

170

Nations and churches die when they only have a heritage. I do not know of a nation on the face of the earth that has a greater heritage than America, except, perhaps, the nation of Israel, but we do not continue in victory as a nation simply because of our heritage. Our problem in this country is not our heritage. Our problem is that God does not mean to us, in this present moment, what He meant to our forefathers.

The same sin exists in the lives of individuals. Some people say, "My dad was a strong Christian. I grew up in a strong Christian home and my parents were great people." That is wonderful, but what is God doing in your life at this moment?

God said, "I want to be memorialized in this way. I am the great 'I AM,' the God of the present." This is the victory. Faith is present tense!

# THE MERCHANT OF CANAAN

What is to be the behavior of the Lord's people? They were in the land of God's choosing for His purpose. What is the Lord's purpose for His people? Hosea 12:6 says, *"Therefore turn thou to thy God: keep mercy and judgment, and wait on thy God continually."* If the Lord is our memorial, we will keep mercy and judgment. This is what God's Word teaches in Micah 6:8, *"He hath shewed thee, O man, what is good; and what doth the LORD require of thee, but to do justly, and to love mercy, and to walk humbly with thy God?"*

Instead of being people of mercy and judgment, the people had become "merchants." God brought them into the land of Canaan, a land of merchants, disease, and devastation, to make a difference. The Canaanites were people who lived wicked lives. They worshiped emblems of sex organs. They were the most debased and defiled people. Instead of being used of God to convert them, God's chosen people were converted by the Canaanites.

171

God's people are in this world to make a difference. To make that difference for God, we must be willing to be different. The goal of God's people is not to be different; it is to be true followers of God, and He makes the difference in our lives.

God sent His people into that land to remove the cancer, and to become a healing to all nations. Instead of going into the land and cutting out the cancer, they went into the land and became infected with the same disease. They had become just like them. Instead of being people of righteous living, mercy, and judgment, they made it their business to be like the Canaanites. They became people full of deceit and oppression. God called them merchants!

*We can be grateful for our heritage, but we must always live the Christian life in the present. God must be real to us at this moment.*

Hosea 12:7-8 says, *"He is a merchant, the balances of deceit are in his hand: he loveth to oppress. And Ephraim said, Yet I am become rich, I have found me out substance: in all my labours they shall find none iniquity in me that were sin."* Ephraim said, "Look at me! I have become rich from these people!" God said, "It was not your responsibility to become merchants and become just like those people. It was your responsibility to make the living God known there, which you did not do."

God does not begrudge us having good things in life that are truly good things. He showers us with those things. His benefits are loaded on us daily. His mercies are new every morning, but He wants His people to understand that we are not here for the same purpose that the rest of this world sees for being here. We are here to make the Lord known. Of course, we ought to work hard and be wise in our dealings; but we are not to live for this world only.

172

In Deuteronomy 8:15-16 we read,

*Who led thee through that great and terrible wilderness, wherein were fiery serpents, and scorpions, and drought, where there was no water; who brought thee forth water out of the rock of flint; who fed thee in the wilderness with manna, which thy fathers knew not, that he might humble thee, and that he might prove thee, to do thee good at thy latter end.*

Deuteronomy 29:5 says, *"And I have led you forty years in the wilderness: your clothes are not waxen old upon you, and thy shoe is not waxen old upon thy foot."* The Lord cared for His people, yet they forsook their faith.

I certainly do not think I am better than anyone else; I am what I am by the grace of God. I remember where God brought me from. I remember the desires God dealt with in my life by giving me other desires, and helping me to desire Him. Without Christ, people are blind and perishing under God's wrath. They are lost and wandering aimlessly through life, finding temporary goals that are meaningless.

Those ancient people who were supposed to know the Lord, and live for Him, said, "Look at us! Look at our benefits! We are rich!" How can anyone truly be rich without God? Let us help people. How are we going to help them? Live the life of a true believer!

Hosea 12:9 says, *"And I that am the LORD thy God from the land of Egypt will yet make thee to dwell in tabernacles."* Ephraim had feasts that they celebrated. During those times of celebration, they would move into tabernacles. They would move into those temporary dwellings and rejoice, thinking about how God had blessed them, and they would remember where God had brought them from. God said to them in a note of mercy and hopefulness, that the day would come again when they would be in tabernacles. He is not necessarily talking about kicking them out. He is talking about the day that would come again when they would celebrate, rejoice, and talk about the goodness of God.

Remember, it is the Lord who gives us the power to get wealth. That is what the Word of God says in Deuteronomy 8:18, *"But thou shalt remember the LORD thy God: for it is he that giveth thee power to get wealth, that he may establish his covenant which he sware unto thy fathers, as it is this day."*

Some of you business people are working very hard and accumulating many possessions. Think of why God has allowed you to do that, because in one moment, the whole picture could change. Remember that blessings come from God.

# THE MINISTRY OF THE PROPHETS

God speaks to us through His Word. God speaks to us through our circumstances. God speaks to us through other Christians. We understand that He spoke through the prophets. Hosea 12:10 says, *"I have also spoken by the prophets, and I have multiplied visions, and used similitudes, by the ministry of the prophets."* God says, "I have spoken unto you, but you did not hear Me." How did the Lord speak? Did He shake the mountain again? God spoke through Hosea, one of His prophets.

Do you recognize the ministry of the prophets? When God's awful acts of judgment are about to fall, we need to hear from Him! God uses the ministry of prophets, those men who thunder forth the Word of God, to do this.

Hosea 12:11 says, *"Is there iniquity in Gilead? surely they are vanity: they sacrifice bullocks in Gilgal; yea, their altars are as heaps in the furrows of the fields."* When men prepared the fields for crops, they took the rocks and piled them up in a certain place so that the ground could be worked for planting. God said, "When I look out across this land, the altars that are to strange gods are as plentiful as the rocks in the fields."

174

The Bible says in Hosea 12:12, *"And Jacob fled into the country of Syria, and Israel served for a wife, and for a wife he kept sheep."* God explained that there was a day when Jacob left the heathen and went to find a believer for a wife.

Hosea 12:13 says, *"And by a prophet the LORD brought Israel out of Egypt, and by a prophet was he preserved."* When the Lord wanted a job done in Egypt, He called His man Moses. He used a prophet.

> *God's people are in this world to make a difference. To make that difference for God, we must be willing to be different.*

Finally, Hosea 12:14 says, *"Ephraim provoked him to anger most bitterly: therefore shall he leave his blood upon him, and his reproach shall his Lord return unto him."* This is something very serious. God concludes these matters and then moves into the thirteenth chapter to talk about death. In the last two words of Hosea 13:1 the Bible says, *"He died."* Before God says, "You are dead," He explains that the same reproach the people had for the things of God would be returned upon them. The way they turned their hearts against God and against the things of God is the same awful thing that was going to be heaped upon them. The reproach would be returned!

How did God start this chapter? His people had the Lord and His blessings. God would have provided all that they needed. They could have fed on the Lord, but instead, they ate the wind. The more they ate the wind and told lies, the more desolation it brought, until finally, God stood over their casket and said, "He is dead."

In the worst of times, we have the greatest message to declare. As believers, we should be so thoroughly identified with Jesus Christ that the same things unbelievers think of Him, they think of us. Let us declare His power to save. God is at work in this world. I want to be in the heart of that work with my Lord. I trust you do too!

175

# CHAPTER THIRTEEN

# THE DEATH AND REBIRTH OF A NATION

 nly God can raise the dead. God's Word tells us in Ephesians 2:1, *"And you hath he quickened, who were dead in trespasses and sins."*

When reading through chapters thirteen and fourteen of the book of Hosea, there is no doubt we are dealing with the death and rebirth of the nation of Israel. In this present moment in which we live, we are privileged to witness what was prophesied more than 2700 years ago coming to pass.

The Bible says in Hosea 13:1-14:9,

> *When Ephraim spake trembling, he exalted himself in Israel; but when he offended in Baal, he died. And now they sin more and more, and have made them molten images of their silver, and idols according to their own understanding, all of it the work of the craftsmen: they say of them, Let the men that sacrifice kiss the calves. Therefore they shall be as the morning cloud, and as the early dew that passeth*

away, as the chaff that is driven with the whirlwind out of the floor, and as the smoke out of the chimney.

Yet I am the LORD thy God from the land of Egypt, and thou shalt know no god but me: for there is no saviour beside me. I did know thee in the wilderness, in the land of great drought. According to their pasture, so were they filled; they were filled, and their heart was exalted; therefore have they forgotten me. Therefore I will be unto them as a lion: as a leopard by the way will I observe them: I will meet them as a bear that is bereaved of her whelps, and will rend the caul of their heart, and there will I devour them like a lion: the wild beast shall tear them.

O Israel, thou hast destroyed thyself; but in me is thine help. I will be thy king: where is any other that may save thee in all thy cities? and thy judges of whom thou saidst, Give me a king and princes? I gave thee a king in mine anger, and took him away in my wrath. The iniquity of Ephraim is bound up; his sin is hid. The sorrows of a travailing woman shall come upon him: he is an unwise son; for he should not stay long in the place of the breaking forth of children.

I will ransom them from the power of the grave; I will redeem them from death: O death, I will be thy plagues; O grave, I will be thy destruction: repentance shall be hid from mine eyes. Though he be fruitful among his brethren, an east wind shall come, the wind of the LORD shall come up from the wilderness, and his spring shall become dry, and his fountain shall be dried up: he shall spoil the treasure of all pleasant vessels. Samaria shall become desolate; for she hath rebelled against her God: they shall fall by the sword: their infants shall be dashed in pieces, and their women with child shall be ripped up.

O Israel, return unto the LORD thy God; for thou hast fallen by thine iniquity. Take with you words, and turn to the LORD: say unto him, Take away all iniquity, and receive us graciously: so will we render the calves of our lips. Asshur shall not save us; we will not ride upon horses: neither will we say any more to the work of our hands, Ye are our gods: for in thee the fatherless findeth mercy.

I will heal their backsliding, I will love them freely: for mine anger is turned away from him. I will be as the dew unto Israel: he shall grow as the lily, and cast forth his roots as Lebanon. His branches shall spread, and his beauty shall be as the olive tree, and his smell as Lebanon. They that dwell under his shadow shall return; they shall revive as the corn, and grow as the vine: the scent thereof shall be as the wine of Lebanon.

Ephraim shall say, What have I to do any more with idols? I have heard him, and observed him: I am like a green fir tree. From me is thy fruit found. Who is wise, and he shall understand these things? prudent, and he shall know them? for the ways of the LORD are right, and the just shall walk in them: but the transgressors shall fall therein.

The Lord said in Hosea 13:14, *"I will redeem them from death."* These last two chapters tell us about the death and rebirth of a nation.

We need to go back in our minds to the beginning of this book of the Bible where the Lord gave us the story of Hosea, Gomer, and their children. Hosea knew that one of the children was not his child, yet he proved his great love to Gomer and those children. The Lord speaks to us and proves His love to us. We build on this story to see God's relationship to His people Israel and His everlasting love for them.

# THE CAUSE OF DEATH

The Lord provides for us here a spiritual autopsy. In this spiritual autopsy, He allows us to walk beside Him and watch as He discovers for us the death of this nation. It is a valuable lesson to learn.

The Bible says in Hosea 13:1, *"When Ephraim spake trembling, he exalted himself in Israel; but when he offended in Baal, he died."* There was a time when Ephraim spoke with such authority that the people trembled. That is all a thing of the past. When he became engaged in idolatry, he died. He lost all power. We are now viewing a lifeless corpse.

*When the Lord is no longer our life, then death has come.*

Hosea 13:2 says, *"And now they sin more and more, and have made them molten images of their silver, and idols according to their own understanding, all of it the work of the craftsmen: they say of them, Let the men that sacrifice kiss the calves."* First they made images to represent only the Lord; but then the images became their gods. They eventually worshiped and kissed those images. Heed this warning! Allow nothing to represent God to you—no images!

Hosea 13:3 says, *"Therefore they shall be as the morning cloud, and as the early dew that passeth away, as the chaff that is driven with the whirlwind out of the floor, and as the smoke out of the chimney."*

The Lord told them they were going to be like the morning cloud, appearing as a vapor and then gone. They were going to be like the early dew—there for a moment and then disappearing. They would be like the chaff—the wind comes and blows it away. They were going to be like smoke from the chimney—it disappears and is gone.

The Lord said they were dead. Examine the body; He shows us the cause of their death. They died when they allowed something to take God's place in their lives. When the Lord is no longer our life, then death has come.

The Bible says in James 1:14-15, *"But every man is tempted, when he is drawn away of his own lust, and enticed. Then when lust hath conceived, it bringeth forth sin: and sin, when it is finished, bringeth forth death."* God says that sin brings forth death.

When God made us, He made us in His image. When Adam and Eve sinned against God, they died spiritually. Spiritual death means separation from God. Physical death means separation from the body.

When we study death in the life of a human being, we understand that a person without God is dead spiritually. The Bible says in Genesis 3:19, *"In the sweat of thy face shalt thou eat bread, till thou return unto the ground; for out of it wast thou taken: for dust thou art, and unto dust shalt thou return."*

Eventually, the body is gone. This does not mean annihilation, because every human being is going to live as long as God lives, either in heaven or in hell. If you do not know the Lord as your Saviour, you are already dead spiritually. To be dead spiritually means that you have no real consciousness of God as the true and living God. Your awareness of God is dead.

When we think about a nation being dead spiritually, we understand that it is dead when there has been a loss of the consciousness of God. There was a time when God was so real to these people in Israel, but now their religion has nothing to do with the true and

181

living God. It does not take much for us to see the parallel between these ancient people and our own land.

When a person begins to die in his soul, something happens to the character of that person. The character is not what it ought to be. Idolatry, putting something or someone before the Lord, always leads to immorality.

When we look at our land, we are witnessing the dying process in the soul of our nation. When death comes to the body, it is gone. Nations crumble and become a part of the dust of the earth. All that is left is a memory of those dead nations.

God stood over Israel and declared, *"He died"* (Hosea 13:1). As this spiritual autopsy is given, God says, "I want you to look at this body of people who once lived and proclaimed the true and living God, who once were people of true faith, character, honesty, decency, and morality. That is all gone! They are dead!"

The cause of death is idolatry taking the place of God. I am not delighted to say that we live in a nation of idolatry. God-forsakers are all around us. The stadiums of our land are filled while churches are neglected. Many professing Christian people will have their children involved in organized sports on the Lord's Day to the neglect of the house of God. Some church leaders say they cannot be in church because their children are playing sports on the Lord's Day. If you are going to lead in God's work, then you must be a leader spiritually and honor the things of God in your life.

We are dying as a nation, yet we act as if this is not really happening. Picture God Himself standing over a nation He loves and has chosen. See Him pronounce their death and perform the autopsy. Then He takes all of us by the hand, leads us to His Word, points us to this dead body, and says, "This is the cause of death. This can be traced back to the place they did not give God in their lives." If you want to know what is wrong with America, you can trace it back to the place that we do not give the Lord in our lives.

# THE CONDITION OF THIS CORPSE

This body is a horrible sight. It is torn into pieces. It is ripped apart. It is in horrible condition. Why does God paint such a gruesome picture of the condition of this corpse? Carefully follow the divine description of this corpse.

The Bible says in Hosea 13:4-5, *"Yet I am the LORD thy God from the land of Egypt, and thou shalt know no god but me: for there is no saviour beside me. I did know thee in the wilderness, in the land of great drought."* God says, "I was there, and I brought you through." He is standing over this lifeless body, and He is about to reveal to us why it is in such a condition. We are going to stand in utter amazement and shock as we see who did this to this body!

Hosea 13:6 says, *"According to their pasture, so were they filled; they were filled, and their heart was exalted; therefore have they forgotten me."* He speaks now as a shepherd. He reveals to us His shepherding work. He guided them, and He gave them Moses to lead them. God is their Shepherd, but they forgot Him.

The Bible says in Hosea 13:7, *"Therefore I will be unto them as a lion: as a leopard by the way will I observe them."* God says, "I will be unto them as a lion who seeks prey to kill and eat." I thought a shepherd was there to protect the sheep? But God declares that He will completely remove His shepherding work. He will take His protecting hand of blessing off. He will allow the enemies to come in.

This body is almost unrecognizable because of the violent death it suffered. Hosea 13:8 says, *"I will meet them as a bear that is bereaved of her whelps, and will rend the caul of their heart, and there will I devour them like a lion: the wild beast shall tear them."* As we look at this corpse, it looks like it has been ripped apart. The vital organs are torn out and savagely destroyed. Can you imagine God speaking like this? Who did this? He says, "I did."

Nations like our beloved America do not die from murder. They die from suicide. God says, "I am going to pull the sheet off now and I want you to look at the body." You will stand in horror. Limbs are torn from the body. The vital organs have been ripped out. There

> Nations like our beloved America do not die from murder. They die from suicide.

has been such a savage attack upon this body. It has been so brutally attacked that no one could imagine this is God's judgment upon His own people. May God apply this to our hearts! Hear the Lord's voice. We must cry out for mercy!

The Bible says in Hosea 13:9, *"O Israel, thou hast destroyed thyself; but in me is thine help."* God stands there looking at this lifeless corpse, crying out for all to hear, *"Thou hast destroyed thyself; but in me is thine help."*

Hosea 13:10-13 says,

> *I will be thy king: where is any other that may save thee in all thy cities? and thy judges of whom thou saidst, Give me a king and princes? I gave thee a king in mine anger, and took him away in my wrath. The iniquity of Ephraim is bound up; his sin is hid. The sorrows of a travailing woman shall come upon him: he is an unwise son; for he should not stay long in the place of the breaking forth of children.*

Now the Lord speaks of an unwise son. The son is passing from a mother's womb to be born, but he refuses to be born. This is dangerous, because the natural process is for the child to pass through the birth canal coming out alive. The unwise son will not break forth.

Then God breaks in again, with a tender heart continuing to interject moments of mercy and pleading. He says in Hosea 13:14,

*"I will ransom them from the power of the grave; I will redeem them from death: O death, I will be thy plagues; O grave, I will be thy destruction: repentance shall be hid from mine eyes."*

The one God loves is dead. Now, by words, He paints a third picture concerning the condition of this corpse. He says in Hosea 13:15-16,

> *Though he be fruitful among his brethren, an east wind shall come, the wind of the LORD shall come up from the wilderness, and his spring shall become dry, and his fountain shall be dried up: he shall spoil the treasure of all pleasant vessels. Samaria shall become desolate; for she hath rebelled against her God: they shall fall by the sword: their infants shall be dashed in pieces, and their women with child shall be ripped up.*

Can you imagine such a horrible thing as infants being broken in pieces? This is a tragic prophecy. Those cruel Assyrians will come in judgment because of the sin of the people, and they will have no mercy. Expectant mothers who are ready to birth a child will be ripped open. The death of the infant is the result of the sin of the mothers and fathers.

I do not know if there could be a more horrible scene for us to look upon than this. God says, "This is the condition of this corpse."

# THE CONFESSION OF SIN

Our Lord will forgive and cleanse when sin is confessed. The Bible says in Hosea 14:1, *"O Israel, return unto the LORD thy God; for thou hast fallen by thine iniquity."* With the expression *"O Israel,"* the Lord is using a term of endearment.

185

My wife and I have had an agreement throughout the years that when we speak to one another, especially about serious things, we will use pet names for each other. We will not simply call out to each other; it is always to be "Darling" or "Sweetheart" The terms of endearment and tones of tenderness are to be voiced. It is not possible to speak harshly when we use soft tones and pet names that are always loving reminders. You see saying, *"O Israel"* is to say, "Oh how I love you."

We witness the great heart of Hosea picturing for us the great heart of God as he cries out through the streets, "Gomer! Gomer, this is your husband. I know you are in sin and living in your whoredoms; but I love you, and I long to embrace you!"

We know that he found her engaged in her whoredoms and actually bought her back from her imprisonment in sin. He paid a ransom to get his own wife back. Our Saviour paid the ransom with His own blood to get us back. He says, *"O Israel, return unto the LORD thy God; for thou hast fallen by thine iniquity."*

Hosea 14:2 says, *"Take with you words, and turn to the LORD: say unto him, Take away all iniquity, and receive us graciously: so will we render the calves of our lips."* He gives us words to speak to our God. Here is true repentance. True repentance is God-ward. True repentance forsakes sin. It is determining in your heart that this sin is never going to be a part of your life again. True repentance appeals to the grace of God. We do not appeal to God's justice. We cry out to God for His mercy and grace. We seek His forgiveness based on the merits of His own Son the Lord Jesus who bled and died for our sin.

The Bible says in Psalms 69:30-31, *"I will praise the name of God with a song, and will magnify him with thanksgiving. This also shall please the LORD better than an ox or bullock that hath horns and hoofs."* The people had been worshiping golden calves, and eventually substituted the calves for God. Now He says, "Our offering, our calves, will be our lips praising Him."

186

In other words, our praise is coming from a heart that is given over to the Lord. When we deal with our sin and acknowledge our sin, appealing to God's grace, God forgives and cleanses, and we must praise the Lord. The forgiven sinner lifts his voice and uses his lips to give glory and honor to the Lord. That is what God wants from His people.

The Bible says in Hosea 14:3, *"Asshur shall not save us; we will not ride upon horses: neither will we say any more to the work of our hands, Ye are our gods: for in thee the fatherless findeth mercy."* Asshur is a primitive name for the capital of Assyria. They had gone to Assyria for help. The Assyrians were going to be the oppressors. They understood now that their help was not in man. There is absolutely nothing of man that can provide what they need.

> *The forgiven sinner lifts his voice and uses his lips to give glory and honor to the Lord. That is what God wants from His people.*

We must come as a nation, as church, and as individuals, recognizing that there is nothing on this earth that can meet the need we have. God allows obstacles in our lives of such insurmountable proportion to convince us of our need for Him.

In Psalm 20:7 we read, *"Some trust in chariots, and some in horses: but we will remember the name of the LORD our God."* Our trust is not in military might. Our trust is in the Lord.

The Bible says in Hosea 14:3, *"Neither will we say any more to the work of our hands, Ye are our gods: for in thee the fatherless findeth mercy."* No more idols for the people of God.

The Bible says in Hosea 14:4-6, *"I will heal their backsliding, I will love them freely: for mine anger is turned away from him. I will be as the dew unto Israel: he shall grow as the lily, and cast forth his roots as Lebanon. His branches shall spread, and his beauty shall be as the olive tree, and his smell as Lebanon."*

Now the Lord tells us of new life. He speaks of rebirth. The Bible says in Hosea 14:7-8, *"They that dwell under his shadow shall return; they shall revive as the corn, and grow as the vine: the scent thereof shall be as the wine of Lebanon. Ephraim shall say, What have I to do any more with idols? I have heard him, and observed him: I am like a green fir tree. From me is thy fruit found."* Ephraim is finished with idols.

Hosea 14:9 says, *"Who is wise, and he shall understand these things? prudent, and he shall know them? for the ways of the LORD are right, and the just shall walk in them: but the transgressors shall fall therein."* The wise will understand things of the Lord.

I do not want to lose hope that God will still send revival to America. The forty-third President of the United States, George W. Bush, was asked by a reporter from a leading newspaper, "I understand you had a private meeting with some conservative Christian people recently and you talked to them about a third awakening. What did you mean by that?"

> *True repentance is God-ward. True repentance forsakes sin.*

The President of the United Sates replied that he had just finished reading a biography of Abraham Lincoln. During Lincoln's life, there was a second Great Awakening, a spiritual revival, in America. The President went on to explain that he was praying and hoping for a third Great Awakening in America. He said, "People everywhere are telling me they are praying for me. I hope that awakening has already started and is on the way."

It is not a political awakening we need. It is not an educational awakening. It is not even a moral awakening. All those things will be affected if we have a true spiritual awakening sent by the Holy Spirit of God. This is what the conclusion of Hosea is all about. It brings us to the mighty moving of God in the world.

How could something so ravaged and horribly destroyed live again? There is only one way. God must breathe life back into it. He is our only hope!

James R. Lowell in his famous poem wrote, "Once to every man and nation, comes a moment to decide." This is our moment!

# For Each Thirteen-Lesson Series

## The Full-Length Book

A beautiful full-length book is published with each thirteen-week series. Teachers will read this book along with their Bible study to prepare for each lesson. Sunday School class members may desire to obtain this book also for further reading. | $12.95

## The Teacher's Guide

The *Teacher's Guide* is a beautifully designed three-ring notebook containing valuable information to assist the teacher in the preparation and presentation of the Bible lesson. Also included are class teaching notes which may be removed from the *Teacher's Guide* and placed in the teacher's Bible to assist him in teaching the lesson. | $12.95

## The Study Guide

This book is to be used by each student in the Sunday School class. It contains helpful summaries of each lesson and provides the student with a place to take notes while the lesson is being taught. Questions are also provided to help the student prepare for next week's lesson throughout the entire week. | $2.95

## Order all three in *The Teacher's Packet*

*at the reduced price of $21.*$^{95}$

The teacher's packet includes the full-length book, the *Teacher's Guide*, and a *Study Guide*. | $21.95

**ORDER Today ONLINE**

*Designed for Sunday School, personal Bible study, and home or office studies.*